SPARKNOTES

Power Tactics

FOR THE NEW SAT

THE MATH SECTION
DATA ANALYSIS,
STATISTICS & PROBABILITY

SPARK
NOTES

A DIVISION OF BARNES & NOBLE PUBLISHING

SPARKNOTES is a registered trademark of SparkNotes LLC

Spark Educational Publishing
A Division of Barnes & Noble Publishing
120 Fifth Avenue
New York, NY 10011

ISBN 1-4114-0279-0

Please submit changes or report errors to www.sparknotes.com/errors

Printed and bound in Canada.

SAT is the registered trademark of the College Entrance Examination Board, which was not involved in the production of, and does not endorse, this product.

Written by Brian Higginbotham

CONTENTS

INTRODUCTION

Truly effective SAT preparation doesn't need to be painful or time-consuming. SparkNotes' *Power Tactics for the New SAT* is proof that powerful test preparation can be streamlined so that you study only what you need. Instead of toiling away through a 700-page book or an expensive six-week course, you can choose the *Power Tactics* book that gets you where you want to be a lot sooner.

Perhaps you're Kid Math, the fastest number-slinger this side of the Mississippi, but a bit of a bumbler when it comes to words. Or maybe you've got the verbal parts down but can't seem to manage algebraic functions. SparkNotes' *Power Tactics for the New SAT* provides an extremely focused review of every component on the new SAT so you can design your own program of study.

If you're not exactly sure where you fall short, log on to **testprep.sparknotes.com/powertactics** and take our free diagnostic SAT test. This test will pinpoint your weaknesses and reveal exactly where to focus.

Since you're holding this book in your hands, it's pretty likely that SAT data analysis, statistics & probability questions are giving you trouble. You've made the right decision because in a few short hours, you will have mastered this part of the exam. No sweat, no major investment of time or money, no problem.

So, let's not waste any time: go forth and conquer SAT data analysis, statistics & probability so you can get on with the *better parts* of your life!

ABOUT THE NEW SAT

THE OLD

The SAT, first administered in 1926, has undergone a thorough restructuring. For the last ten years, the SAT consisted of two sections: Verbal and Math. The Verbal section contained Analogies, Sentence Completions, and Critical Reading passages and questions. The Math section tested arithmetic, algebra, and geometry, as well as some probability, statistics, and data interpretation.

You received one point for each correct answer. For most questions, a quarter of a point was deducted for each incorrect answer. This was called the "wrong-answer penalty," which was designed to neutralize random guessing. If you simply filled in the bubble sheet at random, you'd likely get one-fifth of the items correct, given that each item has five answer choices (excluding student-produced–response items). You'd also get four-fifths of the items wrong, losing $4 \times 1/4$, or 1 point for the four incorrectly answered items. Every time you determined an answer choice was wrong, you'd improve your odds by beating the wrong-answer penalty. The net number of points (less wrong-answer penalties) was called the "raw score."

Raw score = # of correct answers – (1/4 × # of wrong answers)

That score was then converted to the familiar 200–800 "scaled score."

THE NEW

For 2005, the SAT added a Writing section and an essay, changed the name of *Verbal* to *Critical Reading*, and added algebra II content to the Math section. The following chart compares the old SAT with the new SAT:

Old SAT	New SAT
Verbal	**Critical Reading**
Analogies	*Eliminated*
Sentence Completions	Sentence Completions
Long Reading Passages	Long Reading Passages
Paired Reading Passages	Paired Reading Passages
	Short Reading Passages
Math—Question Types	
Multiple Choice	Multiple Choice
Quantitative Comparisons	*Eliminated*
Student-produced Responses	Student-produced Responses
Math—Content Areas	
Numbers & Operations	Numbers & Operations
Algebra I	Algebra I
	Algebra II
Geometry	Geometry
Data Analysis, Statistics & Probability	Data Analysis, Statistics & Probability
	Writing
	Identifying Sentence Errors
	Improving Sentences
	Improving Paragraphs
	Essay
Total Time: 3 hours	*Total Time*: 3 hours, 45 minutes
Maximum Scaled Score: 1600	*Maximum Scaled Score*: 2400 Separate Essay Score (2–12)

The scoring for the test is the same, except that the Writing section provides a third 200–800 scaled score, and there is now a separate essay score. The wrong-answer penalty is still in effect.

NEW PACKAGE, OLD PRODUCT

While the test has changed for test-*takers*, it has not changed all that much from the test-*maker*'s point of view. The Educational Testing Service (ETS) is a not-for-profit institute that creates the SAT for The College Board. Test creation is not as simple a task as you might think. Any standardized test question has to go through a rigorous series of editorial reviews and statistical studies before it can be released to the public. In fact, that's why the old SAT featured a seventh, unscored, "experimental" section: new questions were introduced and tested out in these sections. ETS "feeds" potential questions to its test-takers to measure the level of difficulty. Given the complex and lengthy process of developing new questions, it would be impossible for ETS to introduce *totally* new question types or make major changes to the existing question types.

Now that you know these facts, the "new" SAT will start to make more sense. The changes were neither random nor unexpected. Actually, the only truly *new* question type on the SAT is the short reading passages followed by a couple of questions. However, the skills tested and strategies required are virtually identical to the tried-and-true long reading-passage question type. All other additions to the test consist of new *content* rather than new *question types*. Both multiple-choice and student-produced–response math questions ("grid-ins") now feature algebra II concepts. Same question type, new content. Critical Reading features one fiction passage per test, as well as questions on genre, rhetorical devices, and cause and effect. Same question type, different content.

Even the much-feared new Writing section is in a sense old news. The PSAT and the SAT II Writing test have featured exactly the same multiple-choice question types for years. The essay format and scoring rubric are virtually identical to those of the SAT II Writing test. The College Board had no other choice, given how long the test-development process is.

The other major changes are omissions, not additions: Quantitative Comparisons and Analogies have been dumped from the test.

So, in a nutshell, ETS has simply attached an SAT II Writing test to the old SAT, dropped Analogies and Quantitative Comparisons, added some algebra II content and short reading passages, and ensured that some fiction and fiction-related questions were included. That's it.

A USER'S GUIDE

Reading this book will maximize your score on SAT data analysis, statistics & probability (DS&P) questions. We've divided up your study into two sections: **Power Tactics** and **Practice Sets**. The Power Tactics will provide you with important concepts and the strategies you'll need to tackle DS&P on the SAT. The Practice Sets will give you an opportunity to apply what you learn to SAT questions. To achieve your target score, you'll learn:

- The two question types you'll encounter: multiple-choice and student-produced response, as well as the subtypes: **Graph(ics)**, **Data Puzzlers**, **No Problem with Probability**, and **What the #!*@?**
- What the test-makers are actually trying to test with each DS&P question type.
- Essential concepts and powerful step methods to maximize your score.
- Test-taking strategies that allow you to approach each section with the best possible mindset.
- The 9 most common mistakes and how to avoid them.

In order to get the most out of this book:

- Make sure to read each section thoroughly and carefully.
- Don't skip the Guided Practice questions.
- Read all explanations to all questions.
- Go to **testprep.sparknotes.com/powertactics** for a free full-length diagnostic **pretest**. This test will help you determine your strengths and weaknesses for the entire SAT.
- Go back to our website after you've completed this book to take a **posttest**. This test will tell you how well you've mastered SAT DS&P and what topics you still need to review.

THE POWER TACTICS

ANATOMY OF SAT DS&P

Even without reading this book or preparing for the SAT in any way, you'd still get some DS&P problems right. However, there is a big difference between:

1. Sweating out a problem, breathing a sigh of relief when you finish it, and timidly moving on.
2. Answering a problem, seeing that the next problem contains a cluster of easily interpreted number sets, and hitting a home run on the SAT Math section.

You don't simply want to *survive* the math portion of the SAT, you want to succeed on the test and get a score you—and the colleges you apply to—are happy with. To take your score up to a higher level, you have to do some prep work. The mistake many students make is taking the SAT cold. That's right—no preparation. Not so much as a flip through the information booklet.

By familiarizing yourself with every single type of DS&P question you may encounter on the SAT, you can approach each DS&P question coolly and calmly, knowing in advance what needs to be done to answer it correctly. It's about switching from survival mode to attack mode. It's attack mode that will help you score high.

In this section, we provide you with an X-ray of SAT DS&P. Later on, we'll review the subtypes of questions and specific strategies for approaching each one. By looking at these questions inside and out, you'll know more about how The College Board tests your skills and how to approach each and every question you'll encounter on the test.

There are two types of math questions on the SAT: multiple-choice and student-produced response.

MULTIPLE CHOICE

Here is a typical multiple-choice question and the terms we'll use to refer to its parts:

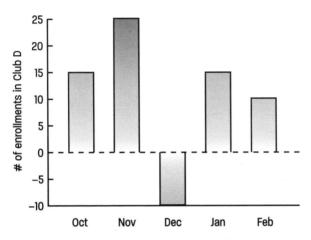

3.   What month saw the greatest increase in enrollments?

(A)   October
(B)   November
(C)   December
(D)   January
(E)   February

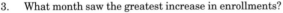

The sentence containing the question is the **stem**. The lettered options below the stem are called the **answer choices**. Numerical answer choices are always listed in order from smallest to largest or largest to smallest. Only one of the answer choices is correct; the other four answer choices are called **distractors**, because that is exactly what they are designed to do—*distract* attention from the correct answer. The stem and answer choices grouped together are called an **item**. An entire multiple-choice section comprised of several items is called a **set**.

STUDENT-PRODUCED RESPONSE

"Student-produced response" is The College Board's way of saying, "Do it yourself, Bub." Simply put, you, the student, must supply the correct answer without choosing from a group of answer choices. Answering student-produced responses requires filling in a grid like the one shown below. Therefore, we refer to these questions as **grid-ins**.

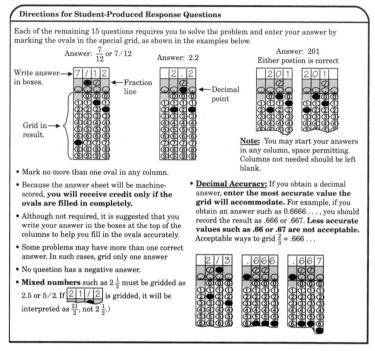

An example of a grid-in might be:

8. The average of $\{7, 8, 10, 12, x, y\}$ is 9.5. What is the average of $x + y$?

The grid is fairly self-explanatory. If you work out an item and the answer is **10**, you write "10" in the spaces and then fill in the "1" oval underneath the 1 and the "0" oval underneath the 0. There are also decimal points and fraction bars in case your answer is not a whole number. We refer to an individual grid-in as an **item**. A complete grid-in section comprised of items is called a **set**.

There are three peculiar things about grid-ins:

1. **There may be more than one correct answer to each item.** You're probably stuck in the "only one correct choice" mindset brought on by excessive multiple-choice preparation. Don't let this paralyze you: if

you get more than one correct answer, pick one, grid it in, and move on to the next item.

2. **Answers can never be negative numbers.** Although there is more than one possible answer, there is actually a limit to what you can grid in. There is no way to denote negative numbers on a grid-in. Why? Who knows, and who cares, for that matter? The fact is that all grid-ins must be positive (or zero, which is neither negative nor positive). So if you come up with more than one correct answer, be sure to choose one that is a positive number. If all your answers are negative, you know you have made a mistake in working out the item.

3. **Improper fractions must be simplified or converted to a decimal answer.** Let's

say came up with $1\frac{1}{2}$ as the answer to an item. If you grid the

answer in as $1\frac{1}{2}$, the computer that scans your answer sheet will

read your answer as $\frac{11}{2}$. To avoid getting this item wrong, convert the

improper fraction into the plain old fraction $\frac{3}{2}$, or the decimal 1.5.

KEY FORMULAS

Math sets on the SAT provide you with key geometric formulas in a reference area that looks like this:

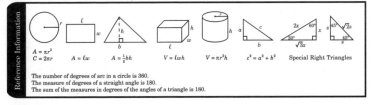

The reference area always appears at the beginning of the set, below the instructions.

WHAT THE SAT COVERS

The DS&P items on the new SAT Math section test the following concepts:

- Statistical analysis
- Graphs, charts, and tables
- Probability
- Permutations and combinations

Don't worry if you don't recognize some of these concepts. That's why you're reading this book! Your job is to master two separate areas of expertise:

1. The concepts listed above, which we'll cover in the Essential Concepts section.
2. The step methods and strategies, which we'll cover in the Essential Strategies section.

ORDER OF DIFFICULTY

The number of an item clues you in to whether it's an easy (low number) or hard (high number) item. Sample items in this book have numbers between 1 and 20 that approximate where the item would appear on a real SAT Math section. Make sure to note the number of the item before tackling it. We cover order of difficulty in more detail in the Test-Taking Strategies section.

ESSENTIAL CONCEPTS

If DS&P were a radio station, this section would be the top-forty count-down. It's not going to include every fact, just the ones that get the most airplay on the test. When we describe a concept, we cover only the DS&P you need to solve SAT items.

You need to have this knowledge down cold. The better you know it, the eas-ier your life will be. Once you're familiar with these concepts, we'll practice applying your knowledge to real SAT items following our specific step methods.

STATISTICAL ANALYSIS

Statistical analysis sounds like some harrowing, difficult course your older brother took his first semester in college. You may be asking your-self, "If college students have difficulty with statistical analysis, how can the SAT expect me, a high school student, to answer these items cor-rectly?" Relax: SAT statistical analysis and college-level statistical analy-sis are two completely different worlds, and we're not just talking about the better parties.

Statistical analysis items on the SAT always include a **data set**, which is a collection of measurements or quantities. An example of a data set is the set of math test scores for 15 students in Ms. Kronhorst's sixth-grade class:

88, 78, 84, 90, 94, 90, 68, 80, 94, 98, 84, 90, 74, 92, 86

You will be asked to find one or more of the following values:

- Arithmetic mean
- Median
- Mode
- Range

Arithmetic Mean, a.k.a. *Average*

When people throw out the word *average* in everyday conversation, they are talking about **arithmetic mean**. Both terms *mean* the same thing. Mean is the most commonly tested statistical analysis concept on the SAT. The actual formula for finding the average is not complicated. It's the sum of all the elements contained in a data set, divided by the number of elements in the set:

$$\text{Arithmetic Mean} = \frac{\text{the sum of the elements of a set}}{\text{the number of elements in the set}}$$

Take another look at the test scores of the 15 students in Ms. Kronhorst's class. We've sorted scores in her class from lowest to highest:

68, 74, 78, 80, 84, 84, 86, 88, 90, 90, 90, 92, 94, 94, 98

To find the arithmetic mean of this data set, sum the scores, then divide by 15, because there are 15 students in her class:

$$\text{mean} = \frac{68 + 74 + 78 + \ldots + 94 + 94 + 98}{15}$$

$$\text{mean} = \frac{1290}{15}$$

$$\text{mean} = 86$$

Unfortunately, the SAT is not going to be this direct when it tests mean. The SAT likes to trick you. Just remember the formula above and the three pieces it is divided into:

• Mean
• Sum of elements
• Number of elements

To solve for any one piece, the other two pieces must be supplied in the item, one way or another. Let's take a look at an example:

4. The average of four numbers is 28. If three of the numbers are 11, 32, and 50, then what is the fourth number?

    (A)   11
    (B)   15
    (C)   19
    (D)   28
    (E)   32

This item appears to be some type of time-consuming, trial-and-error monster in which you begin to choose random numbers to see whether the average will equal 28. But let's take a look at the pieces provided to us in the item. Both the mean and the number of elements are given, and by placing these pieces into the formula above, we come up with the equation:

$$28 = \frac{\text{sum}}{4}$$

$$4(28) = \text{sum}$$

$$112 = \text{sum}$$

In solving this equation, we discover that the sum of the elements must equal 28 × 4, or 112. So if the sum is 112, we can then solve for the fourth number by writing out:

$$11 + 32 + 50 + \text{fourth number} = 112$$

Solving for the fourth number is easy. All you have to do is subtract the sum of 11, 32, and 50 from 112:

$$\text{fourth number} = 112 - (11 + 32 + 50) = 112 - 93 = 19.$$

That's choice **C**.

Always keep in mind that all arithmetic mean items revolve around the three pieces of the formula. Two pieces *must always* be given in some form in order to solve for the third. Once you get this down, you can solve pretty much every item that asks about arithmetic mean on the SAT.

Look at this example:

5. The average of a set of six numbers is 9.5. The average of four of the six numbers is 7. What is the average of the remaining two numbers?

(A)   6
(B)   7
(C)   9.5
(D)   12.75
(E)   14.5

This item seems especially difficult because we aren't given any of the values of the numbers being averaged. So what? We don't need those numbers to solve this item. Because we are looking for the average of two numbers, we only need to know their sum.

If you remember the formula, you'll only need to look at what information is given to you in the item. If the average of six numbers is 9.5, then the sum of the six numbers must equal 9.5 $\times$ 6, or 57. The other information given to you is that the average of four numbers is 7. Therefore, the sum of those four numbers must equal 7 $\times$ 4, or 28. Now, if the sum of all six numbers is 57 and the sum of four of those numbers is 28, then the sum of the remaining two numbers must be 28 + x = 57, or 29. If the sum of two numbers is 29, then their average will be $\frac{29}{2}$, or 14.5. That's choice **E**. Tricky, but doable.

Another tricky mean item the SAT likes to use is the **changing mean**. Those items look like this:

3. The mean age of 8 members of a Dungeons & Dragons club is 18. When a new member joins, the mean age increases to 22. How old is the new member?

    (A)   26
    (B)   34
    (C)   40
    (D)   54
    (E)   67

Remembering the formula, use the information provided in the item to solve for the unknowns. If the average age of 8 members is 18, then the sum of their ages must be 18 $\times$ 8, or 144. When one more member is added, the number of members increases to 9 and our mean increases to 22. Therefore, the new sum of ages must be 22 $\times$ 9, or 198. Because the addition of the new member raised the sum of ages from 144 to 198, the new member's age must be the difference between the two sums, or 54, choice **D**.

Kind of old to be joining a Dungeons & Dragons club, but some people are just late bloomers.

Commit the arithmetic mean (average) formula to memory. Remember, two of the three pieces must be supplied to you in the question. Find out what they are and solve for the third.

Median

Have you ever been on a road trip with your family and noticed a high-way sign that reads "Keep Off the Median"? Did you ever wonder what that meant? On a highway, the median is that strip of grass in the middle separating the two directions of traffic. The **median** serves the same purpose in statistical analysis. It is the middle number in any given data set. Let's look at the hypothetical set Q, which equals $\{12, 5, 7, 4, 5\}$. Rearrange the numbers by order of value, and you get:

$$\text{Set } Q = \{4, 5, 5, 7, 12\}$$

Because there is an odd number of elements, the median is the number directly in the middle, 5.

If a set has an even number of elements, simply take the average of the middle two. For example:

$$\text{Set } R = \{4, 5, 5, 7, 9, 12\}$$

In this case, the middle number is between 5 and 7, so we simply add the two numbers together and divide by 2: $\frac{5 + 7}{2} = 6$. Your median is 6, even though the number 6 doesn't appear in the set.

Mode

The **mode** is the number within a set that appears most frequently. In the set $\{6, 8, 6, 3, 10\}$, the mode is 6 because it appears twice, and all the other numbers appear only once. It is possible to have more than one mode if two or more numbers appear at the same, highest frequency. The set $\{23, 14, 21, 14, 18, 23, 20\}$ has modes of 14 and 23, because both appear twice. In any given set, if all the elements appear an equal number of times, then there is no mode.

Range

The **range** measures the difference between the smallest and largest element of a given data set. Remember the test scores in Ms. Kronhorst's class:

$$\{68, 74, 78, 80, 84, 84, 86, 88, 90, 90, 90, 92, 94, 94, 98\}$$

The range is $98 - 68 = 30$.

GRAPHS, CHARTS, AND TABLES

Visual data can come in many forms, but the SAT focuses on just three types: graphs, charts, and tables. Think of them as the Big Three. Items containing the Big Three come in one of two flavors: Just Read It Vanilla and Chunky Operations Chocolate.

Just Read It Vanilla

On these items, the SAT just tests to see whether you understand the data being presented.

There's nothing controversial or sneaky about these items. The SAT shows you a chart or graph, and you answer a question about the data in the chart or graph. For example:

5. In the following bar graph, the greatest change in the gross national product of Country Z occurred between which two years?

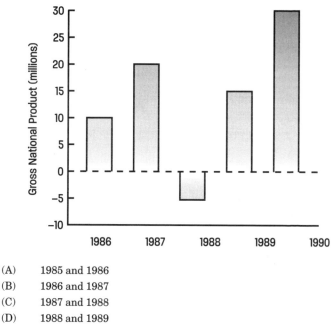

(A)   1985 and 1986
(B)   1986 and 1987
(C)   1987 and 1988
(D)   1988 and 1989
(E)   1989 and 1990

What the heck is "gross national product"? If you don't know, it really doesn't matter. All you need to know is that the bars on the graph represent whatever "gross national product" is, and you're looking for the greatest change between the bars.

A quick look at this graph shows that the three biggest differences appear to be 1987 and 1988, 1988 and 1989, and 1989 and 1990. Because the graph measures the gross national product in increments of 5, you can just count up the amount of change between the years.

- From 1987 (20) to 1988 (–5), there is a difference of 25.
- From 1988 (–5) to 1989 (15), there is a difference of 20.
- From 1989 (15) to 1990 (30), there is a difference of 15.

So the greatest change occurred between 1987 and 1988, choice **C**.

When dealing with graphs and charts, be sure to pay attention to negative and positive values. Also ignore distracting information—such as the meaning of gross national product—that make easy items seem harder.

Chunky Operations Chocolate

These more difficult items ask you to perform some type of operations on data found in a chart, graph, or table, such as calculating a mean or percent. On these items, just reading the information off the graph isn't enough. You have to step into the fray and do a little math grunt work. Wear latex gloves if you're worried about getting your hands dirty, but don't be squeamish. For example, you might be asked something like this:

6.   What was the percent increase in the gross national product from 1986 to 1987?

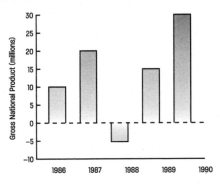

(A)   1%
(B)   50%
(C)   75%
(D)   100%
(E)   125%

First you need to recall the formula for percentage change (check out the *Numbers and Operations* book in this series if you need a review of percents):

$$\text{Percentage change} = \frac{\text{difference}}{\text{original number}} \times 100$$

Let's apply this information to the item. The difference in the gross national product between 1986 (10) and 1987 (20) is 10. Now we divide the difference by the original number. In this case, the original number is 10 (from 1986), the number we increased from to get to 20. So we get:

$$\text{Percentage change} = \frac{\text{difference}}{\text{original number}} \times 100$$

$$\text{Percentage change} = \frac{10}{10} \times 100$$

$$\text{Percentage change} = 1 \times 100 = 100$$

That's choice **D**.

The actual operations you will be performing on the charts and graphs are nothing new, but you will need to be careful when converting the information into mathematical equations.

Double Data Items

The SAT will also require you to interpret and manipulate the data contained in two different graphs or tables. The information you need is going to involve some combination of the graphs and tables.

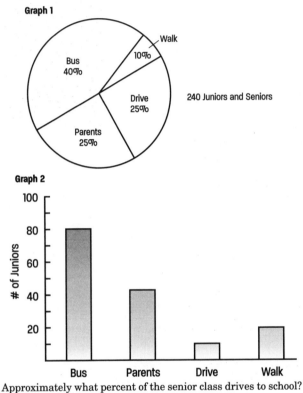

9. Approximately what percent of the senior class drives to school?

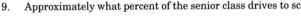

(A)   10.4%
(B)   20.8%
(C)   25%
(D)   40%
(E)   55.6%

The basic question is always: how do the data in the two graphs/tables and the information in the stem relate to one another? From the item, we know we need to figure out the total number of seniors, and the total number of seniors who drive to school. From the tables we know:

1. Total number of juniors and seniors, and the percent of juniors and seniors who drive to school

2. Total number of juniors who drive and the total number of juniors in the school

Now we can find the total number of seniors by adding together the number of juniors (80 + 40 + 10 + 20) and subtracting this sum from the number of juniors and seniors (240):

$$240 - 150 = 90$$

From graph 1 we can determine the total number of juniors and seniors who drive:

$$\frac{25}{100} \times 240 = 60$$

From graph 2 we know that 10 juniors drive to school. Therefore, the number of seniors who drive must be 60 – 10 = 50. Now we have the two pieces of information needed to answer the item. The percent of seniors who drive to school is $\frac{50}{90}$, or 55.6%. That's choice **E**.

Scatterplots

The last type of graph that may appear as an SAT item is the **scatterplot graph**. This is simply a coordinate graph—you know, those graphs with x- and y-axes—with points scattered all over it.

The dots look like a mess, but there's a method to the madness. A general pattern should appear, such that the majority of the points appear clustered around a line or a specific point. It's your job to determine what kind of pattern or trend the points make. You won't be required to do much more than identify whether the points make up a positive, negative, or zero slope. Here is what a typical scatterplot looks like:

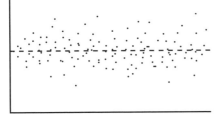

Zero Slope Scatterplot

The points are all over the place, but in general they are clustered around the dotted horizontal line.

PROBABILITY

Probability deals with the randomness of the universe, and this inexact science vainly tries to apply numerical understanding to events that appear to happen in a noncontiguous, nonlinear environment.

What the . . . ?

Oh wait, probability *on the SAT*. That's easy. **Probability** on the SAT is expressed as a fraction. The numerator is the number of times a certain event might occur, and the denominator is the total number of events that might occur. Here is the probability formula you need to know:

$$\text{Probability} = \frac{\text{number of times a certain event might occur}}{\text{total number of events that might occur}}$$

Let's say you're playing a game of High Card with your strange friend Rasputin. High Card is a silly game in which the two of you randomly pick cards from a 52-card deck, and the highest card wins (now that's a Friday night of fun!). You are going to choose from the deck first, and you really want an ace. What's the probability that you will draw an ace?

$$P = \frac{\text{\# of aces}}{\text{total cards}} = \frac{4}{52} = \frac{1}{13}$$

And what's the probability that you'll end up with a non-ace?

$$P = \frac{\# \text{ of non-aces}}{\text{total cards}} = \frac{48}{52} = \frac{12}{13}$$

Here's a more complicated example involving a more exciting Saturday night with toy cars:

9. A certain bag contains five purple toy cars, eight orange toy cars, and seven yellow toy cars. If all the toy cars are placed into a bag, what is the probability that the first car picked will be purple?

(A) $\frac{1}{4}$

(B) $\frac{1}{3}$

(C) $\frac{7}{20}$

(D) $\frac{2}{5}$

(E) $\frac{13}{20}$

There are five ways to pick a purple toy car because there are five different purple toy cars. That's the top number. To find the bottom number, you need to add up all the different cars, regardless of color:

$$5 + 8 + 7 = 20$$

There are a total of 20 different toy cars to choose from in all. Therefore, the probability of picking a purple toy car is:

$$\text{Probability} = \frac{\text{particular outcome}}{\text{total outcomes}}$$
$$\text{Probability} = \frac{5}{20} = \frac{1}{4}$$

That's choice **A**.

When calculating probability, always be sure to divide by the total number of chances. It would have been tempting to leave out the number of purple toy cars in the denominator, because we used them in the numerator, which would have resulted in $\frac{5}{15}$, or $\frac{1}{3}$, an incorrect answer waiting for you among the distractors.

Backward Probability

Backward probability is the basic probability item asked in reverse order. Instead of finding the probability, you are looking for the total, or real number the probability fraction represents. For example:

6. If there are five green toy cars in a bag, and the probability of choosing a green toy car is $\frac{1}{5}$, then how many total toy cars are in the bag?

(A) 5
(B) 10
(C) 15
(D) 20
(E) 25

All you need to do is set up the proper proportional equation. If 1 of 5 toy cars is green and there is a total of 5 green toy cars, then:

$$\frac{1}{5} = \frac{5}{x},$$ where x represents the total number of toy cars.

Now we cross multiply the equation to come up with $x = 25$, choice **E**.

Probability an Event Won't Occur

Certain SAT items will ask about the probability of an event *not* occurring. No sweat. Figure out the probability of the event occurring, and subtract that number from 1:

Probability an event will not occur = 1 – probability an event will occur.

If there is a $\frac{2}{5}$ chance of rain, then the chance of no rain is $1 - \frac{2}{5}$, or $\frac{3}{5}$.

Multiple or Unrelated Probabilities

More difficult probability items deal with multiple related and unrelated events. For these items, the probability of both events occurring is the product of the outcomes of each event:

$P_A \times P_B$, where P_A is the probability of the first event and P_B is the probability of the second event.

A good example of two unrelated events would be: (1) getting heads on a coin toss *and* (2) rolling a 5 with a six-sided die. Just find the probability of each individual event, and multiply them together. There's a 1 in 2 chance of getting heads on a coin and a 1 in 6 chance of rolling a 5. Combining the two gets you:

$$P = P_A \times P_B$$
$$P = \frac{1}{2} \times \frac{1}{6}$$
$$P = \frac{1}{12}$$

The same principle can be applied to find the probability of a series of events. Let's keep it simple and stick to toy cars:

14. Don has a bag of toy cars divided into 8 blue, 9 green, 4 yellow, and 14 red. Sue bets Don a dollar that she can draw 3 green toy cars in a row. What is the probability that Sue will win the bet?

(A) $\dfrac{1}{9}$

(B) $\dfrac{9}{35}$

(C) $\dfrac{12}{935}$

(D) $\dfrac{36}{595}$

(E) $\dfrac{729}{42,895}$

To find the probability of Sue drawing 3 green cars in a row, we need to find the probability of each individual event. The probability of her drawing a green car on her first try is $\dfrac{9}{35}$, because there are 9 green cars and 35 total cars (8 blue + 9 green + 4 yellow + 14 red = 35 total).

The probability of her drawing a green car on the second try is slightly different. With one car already removed from the bag, there are only 34 left, and assuming her first try was successful, there are only 8 green cars left. So the probability of drawing a green car the second time is $\dfrac{8}{34}$. Follow the same procedure for the probability of choosing a green car on the third try, and we come up with $\frac{7}{33}$. So the odds of Sue drawing three green cars in a row is:

$$P = P_A \times P_B \times P_C$$
$$P = \frac{9}{35} \times \frac{8}{34} \times \frac{7}{33}$$
$$P = \frac{3}{5} \times \frac{4}{17} \times \frac{1}{11}$$
$$P = \frac{12}{935}$$

That's choice **C**.

The important point to remember here is that when solving for the probability of a series of events, *always assume that each prior event was successful*, just as we did in the example above.

Geometric Probability

Another difficult concept the SAT might present is **geometric probability**. The same basic concept behind probability still applies, but instead of dealing with total outcomes and particular outcomes, you will be dealing with total area and particular area of a geometric figure. There's nothing fancy here. Just remember this formula and you will be fine:

$$P = \frac{\text{particular area}}{\text{total area}}$$

PERMUTATIONS AND COMBINATIONS

As most high school students correctly suspect, SAT test-makers confine themselves in a dungeonlike environment with a few unfortunate teenage students, poking and prodding them with ideas for the upcoming exam. In this inquisition atmosphere, the darkest region, from which few—if any—students escape, is the Permutations and Combinations Iron Maiden. It is the most gruesome, horrific, and sadistic topic that appears on the SAT Math section. For this reason, permutations and combination items are always considered difficult and, therefore, always appear toward the end of a Math set.

Factorials

The **factorial** of a number, represented by $n!$, is the product of all the natural numbers up to and including n. So if you were asked to find the factorial of 4, it would look like this:

$$4! = 4 \times 3 \times 2 \times 1$$
$$4! = 24$$

The factorial of a number is useful because it expresses the number of ways that n elements of a group can be ordered. So if you had four snow globes from four different cities and you wanted to know how many different ways they could be arranged on your window sill, the answer would be 4!, or $4 \times 3 \times 2 \times 1 = 24$.

Permutations

Permutations also deal with the seemingly countless ways that a certain number of things can be ordered. Let's say we have five students competing in the Olympic sport of underwater basket weaving (this sport doesn't get much airplay). The judges feel that every competitor is a winner in his or her own way and thus ordered five different medals for the five competitors: gold for first, silver for second, bronze for third, iron for fourth, and copper for fifth. How many different arrangements of medal winners could there be? This question is exactly like the snow globe question. We simply take the factorial of 5:

$$5! = 5 \times 4 \times 3 \times 2 \times 1 = 120$$

So there are 120 different arrangements of placing the competitors from first to fifth place.

But let's say that the Olympic Games Committee finds out what the judges are up to and immediately puts a stop to this unfair use of medals, quickly reinstating the standard gold, silver, and bronze medals for the top three competitors, while the last two competitors receive nothing. How many different arrangements of the five competitors could receive the three medals? Now we are dealing with a permutation, which means we need to trot out the following formula:

$$_nP_r = \frac{n!}{(n-r)!}$$

Now, n is the total number of elements (people, snow globes, etc.) that we are dealing with, and r is the size of the subgroup that we are fitting our total elements into—in this case, the subgroup is the number of medals. To find the different arrangements of the five competitors receiving the three medals, we plug 5 and 3 into the equation:

$$_5P_3 = \frac{5!}{(5-3)!} = \frac{5!}{(2)!} = \frac{5 \times 4 \times 3 \times 2 \times 1}{2 \times 1} = \frac{120}{2} = 60$$

Notice that in permutations, *order matters*. In other words, if first and third positions changed with each other and the rest of the order stayed the same, it would still be considered a different arrangement. This is important in order to distinguish between permutations and combinations.

Combinations

A **combination** is an unordered grouping of a set. An excellent example of a combination scenario is when you and your friends order pizza. Whether you order pepperoni, mushrooms, and onions, or you order mushrooms, onions, and pepperoni doesn't matter—it's still the same pizza. The most important thing to remember about combinations is *order does not matter*.

Because the order of the subgroup doesn't matter, the combination solutions will be fewer than the permutation solutions and will be expressed by the following formula:

$$_nC_r = \frac{n!}{r!(n-r)!}$$

The variable n is the total number of elements, and r is the number placed in the subgroups. Let's elaborate on our previous example with the Olympic basket weavers and ask how many different combinations of gold, silver, and bronze competitors are possible. Because it no longer matters who wins the particular medals, we will use the combination formula:

$$_5C_3 = \frac{5!}{3!(5-3)!} = \frac{5 \times 4 \times 3 \times 2 \times 1}{(3 \times 2 \times 1)(2 \times 1)} = \frac{120}{12} = 10$$

There are 10 different combinations of medal winners, or 10 different groups of 3 that would win either gold, silver, or bronze medals, as opposed to 60 different arrangements of individual gold, silver, and bronze winners.

That's it for DS&P. Now that you've mastered these concepts, it's time to show you the best way to put this knowledge to use.

ESSENTIAL STRATEGIES

Before we dive into the step methods and strategies you'll use on the SAT math section, let's first take a look at the types of DS&P items you'll encounter on the SAT.

TYPES OF DS&P ITEMS

On the SAT, the DS&P items are one of four basic types:

- Graph(ics)
- Data Puzzlers
- No Problem with Probability
- What the #!*@?

Graph(ics)

A Graph(ics) item is any item that is accompanied by a graph or chart. The majority of these items simply test whether you can understand and interpret the information being presented to you. These are the Just Read It Vanilla items we covered in the last section. More difficult items will ask you to perform some type of operation on the graph or chart. These are the Chunky Operations Chocolate items.

This is what a typical Graph(ics) item looks like:

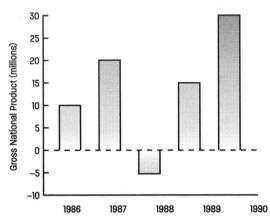

4. What two years had the least difference in gross national product?

(A)   1986 and 1990
(B)   1986 and 1988
(C)   1986 and 1987
(D)   1987 and 1989
(E)   1989 and 1990

Data Puzzlers

Data Puzzler items involve sets of numbers and usually ask about mean, median, mode, range, or any combination of them. The reason we call them *puzzlers* is because the correct answer usually requires you to find some missing piece of information that was not asked about directly. A typical Data Puzzler item will look a lot like this:

7. If the average of 13, 6, 9, x, and y is 12, what is the average of $x + y$?

(A)   6
(B)   9
(C)   12
(D)   16
(E)   32

No Problem with Probability

No Problem with Probability items ask about the chances of a certain event happening or not happening. The majority of answer choices for this item type will be in fraction form:

9. If a card is pulled at random from an ordinary 52-card deck of playing cards, what is the probability of pulling a face card (Jack, Queen, or King)?

   (A) $\dfrac{6}{25}$

   (B) $\dfrac{3}{13}$

   (C) $\dfrac{2}{15}$

   (D) $\dfrac{1}{10}$

   (E) $\dfrac{3}{52}$

What the #!*@?

What the #!*@? items deal with factorials, permutations, and combinations. As we already mentioned, these items almost always appear at the end of Math sets, because they are pretty difficult. A typical What the #!*@? looks like this:

17. Susanne has eleven different medals from her two years of competitive swimming. Unfortunately, the mounting frame she wishes to place them in has room for only two. How many different combinations of medals can Susanne place in her frame?

   (A) 21
   (B) 33
   (C) 55
   (D) 66
   (E) 110

Each of these item types requires a different strategic approach to solve for the right answer. Your goal is to familiarize yourself with both the item type and the strategies that are specific to the particular item.

TACKLING GRAPH(ICS)

You can think of Graph(ics) items as "Eye and Brain" items. First you use your *eyes* to find what is needed, then your *brain* does the rest. Regardless of what the Graph(ics) item specifically asks you to do, always follow this four-step method:

Step 1: Identify the information presented in each graph, chart, or table.

Step 2: Determine what the item wants.

Step 3: Manipulate the graph to find the missing information.

Step 4: Give the item what it wants.

Graph(ics) in Slow Motion

Now let's look at each step more closely, using a graph we are already familiar with:

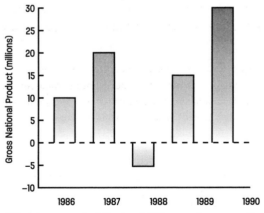

4. What two years had the least difference in gross national product?

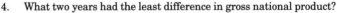

(A)   1986 and 1990
(B)   1986 and 1988
(C)   1986 and 1987
(D)   1987 and 1989
(E)   1989 and 1990

Step 1: Identify the information.

Look at the bar graph and note what information is being presented to you, both horizontally and vertically. For each year given, there is a bar that denotes the amount of the gross national product. Remember that we are not concerned with what "gross national product" means. We care only about the numbers that represent it. Note that the numbers that represent the gross national product are distributed in increments of 5 and that it is possible to have a negative gross national product.

Step 2: Determine what the item wants.

The item is asking for the least difference between any two years. To put it in everyday language: "What two years are closest to the same amount?" Now that we have a clear understanding of what the item wants, let's look back to our bar graph. It's *eye* time!

Step 3: Manipulate the graph to find the missing information.

There isn't a whole lot of manipulation with this straightforward graph item, but go ahead and compare the bars in the graph to one another. At first glance, three particular years seem to be relatively close to the same amount: 1986, 1987, and 1989.

On closer inspection of these three years, the smallest difference appears twice. Between 1986 and 1989 there is a difference of 5, and between 1987 and 1989 there is a difference of 5. Write both these answers down and move on to the next step.

Step 4: Give the item what it wants.

It's not uncommon for the SAT to have more than one correct answer, even on multiple-choice sections, so you need to look at the answer choices and compare them to your answers. Only one, answer choice **D**, matches your answers. The test-makers are sneaky in that they purposely leave out the other correct answer in order for there to be one legitimately correct answer. Instead of getting all worked up over this, just choose the one answer that matches yours and move on. You gave the item what it wanted, end of story. Put it behind you and focus your attention on the next item.

Guided Practice

Try this item on your own.

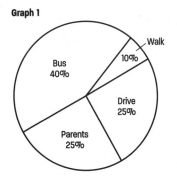

Graph 1

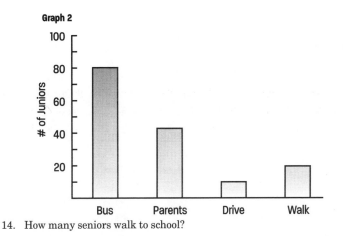

Graph 2

14. How many seniors walk to school?

(A) 4
(B) 8
(C) 10
(D) 16
(E) 20

Step 1: Identify the information.

Don't get overwhelmed because of the multiple graphs and charts. Study each one individually and identify the separate pieces of information presented.

Step 2: Determine what the item wants.

In reading the stem, you'll find that this item is pretty straightforward.

Step 3: Manipulate the graph to find the missing information.

Remember that the SAT wouldn't give you two graphs if you needed only one. How do the two charts relate to each another?

Step 4: Give the item what it wants.

Make sure you answer what the item is actually asking for. Distractors are usually numbers that you use to *work* the solution but are not the correct answer.

Guided Practice: Explanation

Two different graphs and charts? No fear: just use our four-step method to solve this item.

Step 1: Identify the information.

Eye that first pie graph. It shows us the percentage breakdown of how the junior and senior classes get to and from school. It also tells us the total number of students in both classes. The second bar graph displays the actual number of juniors who take the bus, get a ride from their parents, drive, or walk to school.

Step 2: Determine what the item wants.

Fortunately, this item is very direct. We need to find the number of seniors who walk.

Step 3: Manipulate the graph to find the missing information.

From the first graph, we know the percentage of juniors and seniors who walk to school. Now it's time for your brain to do some of the lifting. Because 10% of juniors and seniors walk and there is a total of 240 juniors and seniors, the actual number of walkers would be

$$\frac{10}{100} \times 240 = 24 \, .$$

The second graph only tells us about juniors. But wait: if 20 juniors walk to school, and the total of juniors and seniors who walk is 24, then the number of seniors who walk to school would be: 24 – 20, or 4.

Step 4: Give the item what it wants.

You got this far, now don't blow it by getting cocky. You know 4 is the right answer, but after staring at the graphs for a few minutes, it would be easy enough to choose **C** (10) or **E** (20), because you are familiar with those numbers from solving the problem. You wouldn't believe the number of students who review their practice tests and say, "I got that right, but I chose the wrong answer." The only thing the SAT cares about is the bubbled-in answer choice. No partial credit: it's all or nothing. Be sure to give the item what it wants, answer **A**.

Independent Practice

Look at the following page when you've completed this item.

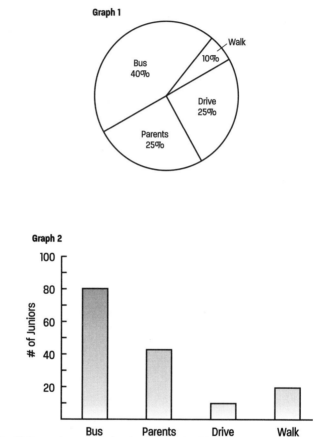

18. If the seniors who take the bus to school began to carpool with their friends and became part of the population that drove to school, then what would be the approximate percentage of juniors and seniors who drove to school?

(A)   19%
(B)   26%
(C)   32%
(D)   37%
(E)   43%

Independent Practice: Explanation

Step 1: Identify the information.

The first pie graph shows us the percentage breakdown of how the junior and senior classes get to and from school. It also tells us the total number of students in both classes. The second bar graph displays the actual number of juniors who take the bus, get a ride from their parents, drive, or walk to school.

Step 2: Determine what the item wants.

This item is specifically asking you to take the number of seniors who ride the bus and add it to the total number of juniors and seniors who drive. Once this is done, you need to figure out the new percentage of drivers.

Step 3: Manipulate the graph to find the missing information.

First, let's find the total number of students who take the bus. It is going to be 40% of the total number of juniors and seniors, $\frac{40}{100} \times 240 = 96$. From the second graph we know that 80 juniors ride the bus, and if 96 juniors and seniors ride the bus, then the number of seniors who ride the bus is 96 – 80, or 16. This is the number we are going to add to our total number of drivers.

Now we need to do the same thing with the drivers in the first graph that we did with bus riders—find the actual number. $\frac{25}{100} \times 240 = 60$. So if there were 60 juniors and seniors driving to school and we added the 16 who used to take the bus, we come up with a new total of 76 drivers.

Step 4: Give the item what it wants.

We are not quite done yet. Remember the item specifically asked for the new *percentage* of drivers after the bus riders were added to them. So now we need to place our numbers into the percentage formula to get

$\dfrac{76}{240} \times 100 \approx 31.67$. Note that the question in the item asks for *approximate*, this simply means to round the answer off some more. That's answer **C**, 32%.

TACKLING DATA PUZZLERS

Use this three-step method every time you answer a Data Puzzler item:

Step 1: Identify and arrange the data according to value.

Step 2: Solve for any missing pieces.

Step 3: Give the item what it wants.

Data Puzzler in Slow Motion
Now let's look at the steps more closely.

7.   If average of 13, 6, 9, x, and y is 12, what is the average of $x + y$?

(A)   6
(B)   9
(C)   12
(D)   16
(E)   32

Step 1: Identify and arrange the data according to value.

We have a set of five numbers, two of which are variables. So let's go ahead and arrange what we can in order according to value. Because we don't know what the variables represent, we'll place them last:

$$\{6,\ 9,\ 13,\ x,\ y\}$$

This ordering probably won't help us too much on an average item, but it's better to be safe than sorry. It would be disastrous to be in the middle of solving an item, only to realize you have to go back to the beginning and start over.

Step 2: Solve for any missing pieces.

Remember the mean/average equation: mean $= \dfrac{\text{sum of all items}}{\text{number of items}}$. On all items involving averages, you need to solve for all three pieces of the equation before moving on to the solution. Any two pieces supplied in the stem will solve for the third. Referring back to the stem, we have five numbers, the average of which is 12. Go ahead and solve for their sum:

$$12 = \frac{\text{sum}}{5}$$
$$\text{sum} = 12 \times 5$$
$$\text{sum} = 60$$

Step 3: Give the item what it wants.

Because the item is asking for the average, we must find the sum of x and y and the number of items being averaged. The second part is pretty easy: x and y are being averaged, so the number of items is 2. To find their sum, we need to add together what we know from the set.

$$6 + 9 + 13 = 28.$$

Now if three of the numbers in the set add up to 28 and the total sum of the set is 60, then the remaining numbers, x and y, must add up to 60 – 28, or 32. We're not quite done yet. 32 looks pretty good, and it's one of the answer choices, but *it's not what the item asked for*. To find their average, divide by 2:

$$\frac{x+y}{2} = \frac{32}{2} = 16$$

The correct answer is **D**, 16.

Guided Practice

Try this next one on your own.

$$\text{Set } B = \{5, 3, x, 5, 11, 8, 9\}$$

10. If the median of set B is also its average, then what is one possible value of x?

(A)   5
(B)   8
(C)   11
(D)   15
(E)   21

Step 1: Identify and arrange the data according to value.

Are the numbers in this set in no particular order? You know what to do.

Step 2: Solve for any missing pieces.

Is mean/average involved in the item? If so, find all three parts to the equation.

Step 3: Give the item what it wants.

Make sure you have the number the item asked for and not a distractor.

Guided Practice: Explanation

Step 1: Identify and arrange the data according to value.

There are seven numbers all jumbled together in set B, so let's put those in order.

$$\{3, 5, 5, 8, 9, 11, x\}$$

Because x is unknown, we went ahead and placed it after the 11. This does not mean that x is greater than 11. Realistically, x could rightfully be placed anywhere within the set.

Step 2: Solve for any missing pieces.

Here is where the item becomes a little tricky. We know the average has to equal the median, so let's take a look at what the possible medians of set B could be. If x is removed from the set, then the two possible medians are 5 and 8.

Let's start with 5. If 5 is the median, then 5 must also be the average. If 5 is the average, then the sum of all 7 numbers in the set must be 5×7, or 35. If the sum of all seven numbers is 35, then the solution for x would look like this:

$$3 + 5 + 5 + 8 + 9 + 11 + x = 35$$
$$41 + x = 35$$
$$x = -6$$

Let's look at 8. If 8 is the median, then 8 must also be the average. If 8 is the average, then the sum of all 7 numbers in the set must be 8×7, or 56. If the sum of all seven numbers is 56, then the solution for x would look like this:

$$3 + 5 + 5 + 8 + 9 + 11 + x = 56$$
$$41 + x = 56$$
$$x = 15$$

Step 3: Give the item what it wants.

We have discovered two possible values for x. Let's see if any of them match up with the answer choices. Bingo! Answer choice **D** is 15. Don't worry about the –6; the item asked for one *possible* answer choice. Choose **D** and move on.

Independent Practice

Work out this item on your own. Then turn the page for an explanation.

14. The average test score of six students is 96. What would a seventh student need to score to reduce the average to 89?

(A)   35
(B)   47
(C)   55
(D)   89
(E)   95

Independent Practice: Explanation

Step 1: Identify and arrange the data according to value.

The data for this item are the unknown test scores of six students. Because there is no way of determining what they are, it is impossible to arrange them in any order. Let's move on to step 2.

Step 2: Solve for any missing pieces.

We do know that the item involves averages, so let's look for the pieces to the average formula and solve for any missing information. Because 96 is the average of six students' test scores, we can solve for the sum of all their test scores:

$$96 = \frac{\text{sum}}{6}$$

$$\text{sum} = 96 \times 6$$

$$\text{sum} = 576$$

The second part of the stem informs us that an additional student takes the test—increasing the number of test-takers to seven—and changes the average to 89. So the sum of all seven test-takers must now equal:

$$89 = \frac{\text{sum}}{7}$$

$$\text{sum} = 89 \times 7$$

$$\text{sum} = 623$$

Step 3: Give the item what it wants.

The item asks for the test score of the seventh test-taker. If the sum of the previous six test-takers is 576 and the sum of the previous six plus the additional seventh is 623, then the additional test-taker's score would have to be the difference between 623 and 576. 623 – 576 = 47, answer **B**.

TACKLING NO PROBLEM WITH PROBABILITY

As confusing and frustrating as these items can get, they can be easily managed if you learn to employ the three-step method described below:

Step 1: OVER—Identify the number of outcomes that fit the item's requirements.

Step 2: UNDER—Identify the total number of outcomes possible.

Step 3: Place the OVER over the UNDER. Give the item what it wants.

No Problem with Probability in Slow Motion

Now let's look at the steps more closely, starting with a fairly common probability item.

9. If a card is pulled at random from an ordinary 52-card deck of playing cards, what is the probability of pulling a face card (Jack, Queen, or King)?

(A) $\frac{6}{25}$

(B) $\frac{3}{13}$

(C) $\frac{2}{15}$

(D) $\frac{1}{10}$

(E) $\frac{3}{52}$

Step 1: OVER—Identify the number of outcomes that fit the item's requirements.

Be careful: you don't want to jump in too fast and say 3. In an ordinary deck of playing cards, each card appears one time for each of the four suits. Therefore, the total number of outcomes that fit the requirements is 12, four suits for each of the three face cards.

Step 2: UNDER—Identify the total number of outcomes possible.

If you are pulling a card at random from a 52-card deck, then there are 52 total outcomes possible.

Step 3: Place the OVER over the UNDER. Give the item what it wants.

Create a fraction with the numbers you came up with for OVER and

UNDER. $\frac{12}{52} = \frac{3}{13}$, answer **B**.

Guided Practice

Try this one on your own.

15. Count Chocula's "trick-or-treat" bag has eight pieces of chocolate, five pieces of gum, and three jawbreakers. If two pieces are chosen at random, what is the probability that both are chocolate?

(A) $\frac{3}{4}$

(B) $\frac{1}{2}$

(C) $\frac{7}{15}$

(D) $\frac{1}{4}$

(E) $\frac{7}{30}$

Step 1: OVER—Identify the number of outcomes that fit the item's requirements.

Is there more than one probability here?

Step 2: Under—Identify the total number of outcomes possible.

Think carefully about all the possibilities.

Step 3: Place the OVER over the UNDER. Give the item what it wants.

Do you remember what to do to find the probability of multiple events?

Guided Practice: Explanation

This is a variation on the standard probability item. You still want to follow the basic steps, but notice how they slightly differ.

Step 1: OVER—Identify the number of outcomes that fit the item's requirements.

Because the item asks about multiple events, we need to find the probability of each individual event first. The first time a piece of candy is picked from the bag, how many are chocolate? 8. Hold on to this number, we'll come back to it. The second time a piece of candy is picked from the bag how many pieces of chocolate will there be (always assume the previous trials were successful)? 7. That's it for step 1.

Step 2: UNDER—Identify the total number of outcomes possible.

This is the exact same thing we did in step 1, but now we are concerned only with the total pieces of candy. The first time a piece of candy is picked there is a total of 16 pieces, but the second time the total changes to 15. Keep these numbers handy.

Step 3: Place the OVER over the UNDER. Give the item what it wants.

Combine the numbers you came up with to create two probabilities. The probability of getting a piece of chocolate the first time is $\frac{8}{16} = \frac{1}{2}$. The probability of getting a piece of chocolate the second time would be $\frac{7}{15}$. To find the probability of these two events happening consecutively—in a row—just multiply them together:

$$\frac{1}{2} \times \frac{7}{15} = \frac{7}{30}$$

Answer **E** is correct.

Independent Practice
Once you've completed this item, turn the page for the solution.

19. A coin is flipped three times. What is the probability that it will land on heads at LEAST once?

(A)   0

(B) $\frac{1}{8}$

(C) $\frac{3}{8}$

(D) $\frac{7}{8}$

(E)   1

Independent Practice: Explanation

This item is one of the more difficult probability items you're likely to encounter on the SAT. But you still want to stick with our trusty three-step method.

Step 1: OVER—Identify the number of outcomes that fit the item's requirements.

All right, the stem asks for heads coming up *at least* once, so this means we need to include the probability of getting one head, two heads, and all three heads, as well as any of the different orders in which they can appear in three tosses. That's a lot of thinking, and with the time constraints of the test, you're not going to have enough time to write out all the different outcomes where you get at least one head.

Let's try approaching this item with a little creativity. The stem asks for *at least* one head, but consider the opposite of this stem—What would be the probability of NO heads?—which is the same as asking for the probability of all tails. Looking at the item this way, we can identify the number of outcomes in which we get all tails. There is one chance on the first toss, one chance on the second toss, and one chance on the third toss.

Step 2: UNDER—Identify the total number of outcomes possible.

Whenever we toss a coin, there are only two possible outcomes. Because all three tosses are independent of one other—that is, the coin is picked up and tossed again—our total outcomes for each individual toss is 2.

Step 3: Place the OVER over the UNDER. Give the item what it wants.

To determine the probability of multiple events, you need to multiply the probability of each individual event together. So the probability of getting tails on all three tosses—which is the same as never getting heads—would be $\frac{1}{2} \times \frac{1}{2} \times \frac{1}{2} = \frac{1}{8}$. Don't be fooled by answer choice **B**, $\frac{1}{8}$. The item did not ask for the probability of tossing tails three times. The item asks for the probability of tossing *at least* one head, which is the same as *not* tossing three tails. Now we subtract the probability of three tails from

1, and the result is the probability of tossing *at least* one head.

$1 - \dfrac{1}{8} = \dfrac{7}{8}$, answer **D**.

TACKLING WHAT THE #!*@?

Permutation and combination items are the test-makers' last-ditch effort to bring down your score. The test-*takers'* usual reaction to these items is "What the #!*@?" Believe it or not, this visceral reaction can actually help you identify a permutation or combination item. When you find yourself frustrated beyond belief, there is a very good chance you're looking at one of these items.

Once you've collected yourself, follow the three-step method below for solving What the #!*@? items. Not only will it lead you to the correct answer but to a new found feeling of empowerment from shredding the SAT math section.

Step 1: Does order matter? If YES, go to step 2 ONLY. If NO, go to steps 2 and 3.

Step 2: Multiply the factorial of the number of things being arranged to the number of spaces designated for arrangement.

Step 3: Divide by the factorial of the number of spaces in the group.

What the #!*@? in Slow Motion

Now let's look at the steps more closely, starting with a fairly common What the #!*@? item.

17. Susanne has eleven different medals from her two years of competitive swimming. Unfortunately, the mounting frame she wishes to place them on only has room for two. How many different combinations of medals can Susanne place on her frame?

   (A)   21
   (B)   33
   (C)   55
   (D)   66
   (E)   110

Step 1: Does order matter? If YES, go to step 2 ONLY. If NO, go to steps 2 and 3.

Susanne is placing two medals onto a mounted frame. Does it matter in which order the medals are placed? No, the word *combinations* in the item tells us that order does not matter. Recall from our study of the essential concepts that combinations deal with groups of things, while permutations deal with arrangements. In permutations, order matters.

Now let's move on and complete steps 2 and 3.

Step 2: Multiply the factorial of the number of things being arranged to the number of spaces designated for arrangement.

This step is actually easier than it sounds. How many medals does Susanne have to arrange? 11. How many spaces on her frame does she have for arrangement? 2. So all we do is multiply the first two values in the factorial of 11 (11!):

$$11 \times 10 = 110$$

Susanne has 11 medals to choose from for the first space and 10 to choose from for the second space.

Step 3: Divide by the factorial of the number of spaces in the group.

Because there are two positions on the frame, we go ahead and divide by the factorial of 2, (2!). So now our entire equation looks like this:

$\frac{11 \times 10}{2 \times 1} = \frac{110}{2} = 55$. That's it, that's all! The correct answer is **C**, 55.

Guided Practice

Try this one on your own.

17. Kevin had a very busy Saturday afternoon. He just bought a new spice rack that holds four spice jars. When he got home, he remembered that he has six different types of spices. How many different arrangements of spices, from left to right, are possible for Kevin's new spice rack?

(A)   15
(B)   60
(C)   120
(D)   180
(E)   360

Step 1: Does order matter? If YES, go to step 2 ONLY. If NO, go to steps 2 and 3.

Is the item asking about groups or arrangements? If it is a group, then order does not matter. If it is not a group, then it must be an arrangement, and order does matter.

Step 2: Multiply the factorial of the number of things being arranged to the number of spaces designated for arrangement.

Remember your factorials. Find the number of spaces in the arrangement or group.

Step 3: Divide by the factorial of the number of spaces in the group.

How many people or things are in the group? That is the number you'll use to create a factorial.

Guided Practice: Explanation

Step 1: Does order matter? If YES, go to step 2 ONLY. If NO, go to steps 2 and 3.

The item is asking for arrangements, from left to right. This means that order does matter. Now we go to step 2 *only*.

Step 2: Multiply the factorial of the number of things being arranged to the number of spaces designated for arrangement.

How many things are being arranged? Six spices. How many spaces on the spice rack are there for them? Four. Now multiply the factorial of the number of spices (6!) down to the number of spaces available. It should look like this:

$$6 \times 5 \times 4 \times 3 = 360$$

That's the number of arrangements, answer **E**. I hope Kevin doesn't ask us to help.

Step 3: Divide by the factorial of the number of spaces in the group.

This step isn't necessary for this item, so move on.

Independent Practice

The explanation for this item is on the following page.

18. The student council has five vacancies since the seniors graduated. Nine talented and aspiring young freshmen have applied to fill the vacancies. How many different groups of freshmen are possible to fill the vacancies?

(A)   60
(B)   120
(C)   126
(D)   7,560
(E)   15,120

Independent Practice: Explanation

Step 1: Does order matter? If YES, go to step 2 ONLY. If NO, go to steps 2 and 3.

The key word in this item is *groups*, which tells us that order does not matter. On to steps 2 and 3.

Step 2: Multiply the factorial of the number of things being arranged to the number of spaces designated for arrangement.

How many people or things are being arranged? Nine freshmen. How many spaces are there on the student council for them? Five. The factorial of 9, (9!), multiplied down five spaces looks like this:

$$9 \times 8 \times 7 \times 6 \times 5$$

Step 3: Divide by the factorial of the number of spaces in the group.

How many freshmen are going to be in the group? Five. So we are going to divide by the factorial of 5, (5!). Here's our entire equation:

$$\frac{9 \times 8 \times 7 \times 6 \times 5}{5 \times 4 \times 3 \times 2 \times 1} = \frac{15120}{120} = 126$$

That's it! There is the possibility of 126 groups of 5 freshmen to fill the vacancies of the student council. Our answer is choice **C**, 126.

TEST-TAKING STRATEGIES

In addition to all the DS&P concepts and step methods you have learned, you must also arm yourself with some broad SAT test-taking strategies. If you don't have the correct overall approach to the SAT, all the DS&P work you have done in this book will fall by the wayside.

Have you ever showed up alone at a house party after it already started? It can be pretty intimidating. Groups of kids in all the rooms and on the front and back lawns. Your instinct is to walk through the entire house and find your group of friends first. After you talk with your friends for a while and get relaxed, you start to wander through and begin to talk with and meet new people. You would never just arrive and try to talk with new people immediately—that's social suicide.

PACING

Approach every SAT Math section like this party. First, get relaxed and comfortable by answering the items that you are familiar with. Jump around through the section and look for them. There is no rule that says you must answer the items in order. After you have answered all the items you are comfortable with, branch out and try the ones you are unfamiliar with.

This process is made easier by the fact that every Math section is set up by order of difficulty. The first item is the easiest, the next item is a tiny bit tougher, and so on until the end. A typical 20-item Math set breaks down the following way:

Difficulty	Item Number
Easy	1–6
Medium	7–14
Hard	15–20

Keep this chart in mind as you take practice tests, but also remember that the order of difficulty is simply based on what the test-makers consider to be easy, medium, and hard. You are your own person, and you may find item 15 to be much easier to complete than item 5.

Answering every problem in order—no matter how long it takes—is a classic SAT mistake. Students start with item 1 and then just chug along until time is called. Don't be that chugger! If an item takes more than a minute to solve, skip it and move on to the next item. The goal on the first run-through of an SAT Math section is to find the items with which you are most comfortable. Save the other items for your second go-around. Although the next item is statistically a little tougher, you might find them easier to answer.

THE SAT IS NOT A NASCAR-SANCTIONED EVENT

The SAT is a timed test, and some people take this to mean they should answer items as quickly as possible. They cut corners on items to speed through a section. This is a classic error, and it's an especially disastrous policy on SAT Math, since the "easiest" items are at the beginning. If the last item had a fifty-point bonus attached to it, things would be different, but every item counts the same. Getting two hard items right won't do you any good if you missed two easy items in your haste. You'll be better off answering the easy items correctly and then using whatever time you have left to take an educated guess at the remaining harder items.

Accuracy counts more than speed. First, go through a section and answer all the items that come easily to you. Then:

- Take the time to answer every one of these items *correctly*.
- Take another shot at the remaining items during the second run-through. If you spend two minutes, and the item still doesn't yield an answer, take a guess and move on.

To achieve the second point, avoid choosing the answer that looks "right" at first glance. On easy items, this choice may well be the correct answer. For items numbered 12 or higher, an answer that screams "Ooh! Ooh! Pick me and hurry on!" should also be handled like a live snake. SAT distractors are designed to catch students in a hurry. More often than not, an answer choice for a hard item that looks too good to be true is exactly that—*too good to be true.*

Remember, if you can safely eliminate one of the answer choices as being wrong, you should take a guess because you may beat the wrong-answer penalty.

For most students, the best method for picking up points in the Math section is by:

- Answering all the easy questions correctly.
- Slowing down and catching most of the medium items.
- Getting 25–50% of the hard items.

This approach is not as thrilling as getting the hardest five items right (while making tons of mistakes along the way), but it does put you on the best path to a high score. Besides, do you really think the SAT can be thrilling?

WEAR YOUR NO. 2 DOWN TO A NUB

There are many students who are afraid of placing a smudge on their test booklets. These students don't write down any formulas or equations. They don't write out their work when manipulating numbers. They don't score very well on the SAT either.

Get over your respect for the SAT test booklet. Write all over those rough, recycled pages. When you are finished, your test booklet should be covered with scrawls, notes, computations, and drawings. In fact, the simple act of writing something down for every item helps improve your SAT score. It forces you to put your thoughts down on paper instead of trying to solve items in your head. If you try to answer items in your head, the SAT chews you up and spits you out.

Be a smart test-taker and jot down everything you can.

TAKE A DEEP BREATH AND . . .

Don't freak out when you take the SAT. Sure, the test is important, but many people act as if their entire lives depend on how they do on this one exam. It's just one test, and you can even take it over again.

On test day, you want to sit down feeling confident and positive. Do what you have to do to get in that mindset—wear a lucky bracelet, do a hundred pushups, write love poetry—because you need to believe in yourself when taking on the SAT. A positive outlook increases your willingness to take an educated guess on a tough probability item instead of leaving it blank. It helps you trust inner ear, enabling you to answer a grammar item, even though you don't know the grammatical rule being tested. A positive approach to the SAT is more important than any single fact or strategy you could learn. Banish anxiety from your mind, and all the skills and strategies you've learned to prepare for the SAT will take its place.

THE 9 MOST COMMON MISTAKES

As you prepare, keep the following common mistakes in mind. Some are mistakes to avoid when taking the actual test. Others are mistakes to avoid during your preparation for the test.

1. Forgetting the basic formulas that are associated with DS&P. (Know these formulas!)
2. Forgetting to look for the hidden, unstated pieces of the puzzle that hold the key to an item.
3. Trying to work an item in your head instead of writing your work down.
4. Not picking the answer the item asks for. Are you falling for a distractor?
5. Failing to work through the practice sets in this book—*reading* the book is not enough.
6. Failing to practice the step methods on every practice item. You need these methods when the answer isn't obvious to you.
7. Refusing to guess after eliminating one or more answer choices.
8. Answering every item in order.
9. Rushing through a set instead of thinking each item through.

CONCLUSION

Without practice, you won't master SAT DS&P. You've learned quite a bit since you picked up this little book, but now comes the hard part—*you* have to apply it to testlike items. There are two practice sets at the end of this book: one made up of multiple-choice items and one made up of grid-ins. Here are some tips for getting the most out of these items.

- **Do not time yourself on the first practice set.** When you begin, don't worry about time at all. Take as long as you need to work through each set.

- **Read the explanations for all items, regardless of whether you got them right or wrong.** This is critical—always read *all* the explanations for each set's items. The idea is to develop skills that help you score points as quickly as possible. Most important, scoring a point doesn't mean you got it in the most efficient manner. The overarching goal is to *apply* the methods you've learned. Whether you get all, some, or none of the practice items right doesn't matter.

After the first set, you may want to start paying attention to time. Certainly by the actual test, give yourself about a minute or so per item.

All the vital information and snazzy strategies you learn in this book won't do a lick of good if you don't use them on the day of the test. Sadly, this happens more often than you might think. Students acquire useful tips, but once the test starts Saturday morning, all of it goes out the window.

To help ensure that this doesn't happen to you, tackle these two sets *using the skills and strategies you just learned.* Don't worry about how many you get right or wrong: they're just practice sets. Instead, focus on how well you use the techniques you learned. When you look at a DS&P item, can you tell what type of item it is? If it's a Data Puzzler, did you remember to arrange the values from smallest to largest? If it's a What the #!*@?, are you dealing with a permutation or a combination?

Don't get frustrated by your progress on the practice sets. Every mistake you make on the practice sets is one that you will avoid on the real test. Yes, there are some DS&P rules you don't know, but learning about these on practice items corrects that deficit. When the real SAT rolls around, you'll have yet another DS&P fact in your arsenal that you can employ if needed.

ADDITIONAL ONLINE PRACTICE

Once you're done working through the items and explanations in this book, you can practice further by going online to **testprep.sparknotes.com** and taking full-length SAT tests. These practice tests provide you with instant feedback, delineating all your strengths and weaknesses.

Also, be sure to take the free DS&P posttest to see how well you've absorbed the content of this book. For this posttest, go to **testprep.sparknotes.com/powertactics**.

FINALLY . . .

The goal of this book is to show you effective methods for answering SAT DS&P items. We hope this helps strip away some of the mystery about the SAT that causes so many students to freak out on test day. You should realize that the SAT is not a perfect indicator of your math ability. In fact, it simply tests your knowledge on a narrow range of math topics. Master those topics, and you will conquer the SAT.

On to the practice items!

THE PRACTICE SETS

PRACTICE SET 1: MULTIPLE CHOICE

Questions 1 and 2 refer to the following graph.

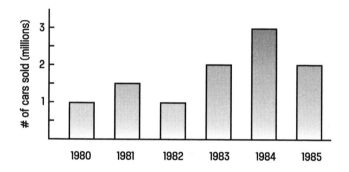

1. According to the information in the graph, what year saw a decrease in the number of cars sold?

    (A) 1980
    (B) 1981
    (C) 1982
    (D) 1983
    (E) 1984

2. According to the information in the graph, in what two years were the number of cars sold closest to equal?

    (A) 1980 and 1981
    (B) 1981 and 1982
    (C) 1981 and 1983
    (D) 1983 and 1985
    (E) 1984 and 1985

Question 3 refers to the following set.

Set A {6, 8, 3, 2, 3, 5, 9, 5, 12, 3, 9, 1, 1, 6, 7}

3. The numbers in set A represent the amount of money in dollars that 15
students brought to school. Which of the following is the median amount
of money the students brought to school?

(A) 3
(B) 5
(C) 6
(D) 7
(E) 8

Questions 4 and 5 refer to the following graph.

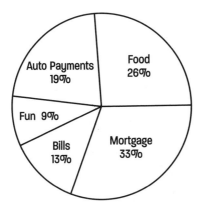

Monthly Household Income = $2,400

The pie chart above represents the monthly distribution of family X's income.

4. According to the graph, how much is family X's mortgage in dollars?

(A) 216
(B) 312
(C) 456
(D) 624
(E) 792

5. If family X completed all its car payments and transferred all the auto money into the "Fun" budget, then family X would most nearly spend the same amount on fun as they spend on

(A) food
(B) mortgage
(C) bills
(D) food and bills
(E) food and mortgage

Set D {9, 11, 6, x, x}

6. In set D above, what is the value of x if the average of the five numbers is 8?

(A) 4
(B) 7
(C) 8
(D) 10
(E) 14

Set G {5, 8, 13, x, y}

7. If x and y are distinct positive integers and the average of set G is 6.8, then which of the following could be the mode of set G?

(A) 13
(B) 11
(C) 9
(D) 8
(E) 5

8. A certain deck of cards consists only of 10's, Jacks, Queens, and Kings, and is divided up evenly in a 52-card deck. What is the probability of not drawing a Jack?

(A) $\frac{1}{4}$

(B) $\frac{1}{3}$

(C) $\frac{1}{2}$

(D) $\frac{2}{3}$

(E) $\frac{3}{4}$

Questions 9 and 10 refer to the following graph.

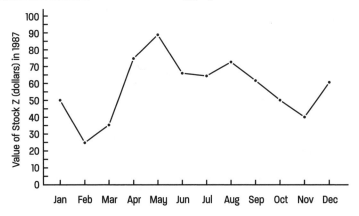

The graph shows the values of Stock Z for the year 1987.

9. The greatest increase for Stock Z, compared to the month before, occurred during which month?

   (A) April
   (B) May
   (C) December
   (D) March
   (E) August

10. For the overall year, 1987, what was the percent increase of Stock Z?

   (A) 250%
   (B) 100%
   (C) 50%
   (D) 20%
   (E) 0%

Question 11 refers to the following graph.

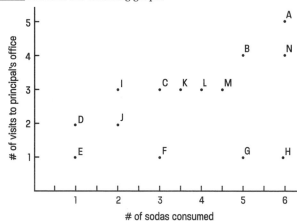

# of sodas consumed

Of all the students sent to the principal's office on one school day, each was asked his/her soda consumption for that day. The graph above represents each child's answer.

11. If you were to draw a line showing the average ratio of principal's office visits to sodas consumed, this line would most likely pass through point

   (A) K
   (B) I
   (C) H
   (D) G
   (E) F

12. The average income of Ironville, Pennsylvania, is $24,000 a year. A new mill has brought in six new incomes that increase the average to $32,000. If there were initially eight incomes in Ironville, what is the average income of the six new families?

   (A) $42,666.67
   (B) $74,666.67
   (C) $106,666.67
   (D) $192,000.00
   (E) $256,000.00

13. In a certain bag of candy-coated chocolates with peanut centers, seven
    are yellow, three are red, five are blue, five are brown, and eight are
    green. If two candies are chosen at random, what is the probability that
    the first is green and the second is red?

    (A) $\dfrac{1}{30}$

    (B) $\dfrac{11}{28}$

    (C) $\dfrac{2}{63}$

    (D) $\dfrac{3}{98}$

    (E) $\dfrac{1}{10}$

Questions 14 and 15 refer to the following graph.

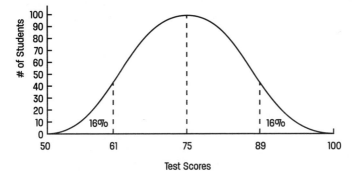

14. What percent of the students scored between 61 and 89?

    (A) 2%
    (B) 14%
    (C) 50%
    (D) 68%
    (E) 74%

15. What are the mean, median, and mode, respectively, of the test scores?

    (A) 89, 80, 75
    (B) 75, 75, 75
    (C) 61, 75, 89
    (D) 89, 75, 61
    (E) 75, 61, 89

16. Iron Chef is preparing an eclectic six-course meal to consist of shrimp cocktail, mango salad, miso soup, stir-fried eggplant, turducken (chicken stuffed into a duck stuffed into a turkey), and a chocolate éclair. Disregarding all formality to the traditional order of the courses, in how many different orders can the courses be presented?

(A) 240
(B) 440
(C) 720
(D) 1,440
(E) 1,640

Questions 17 and 18 refer to the following graph.

Distribution of Profits for Company X

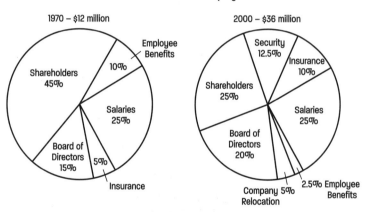

17. In 2000, Company X had to add security costs and company relocation to its profit distribution. These expenses were taken out of employee benefits. What was the approximate percent decrease in employee benefits from 1970 to 2000?

(A) 7.5%
(B) 17.5%
(C) 25%
(D) 33.3%
(E) 35%

18. If the Board of Directors consists of the same eight people for both 1970 and 2000, then between 1970 and 2000, each board member, on average, saw his or her portion of profits increase by how much?

    (A) $225,000
    (B) $675,000
    (C) $900,000
    (D) $1,200,000
    (E) $1,800,000

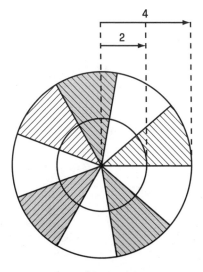

Note: all 9 arc sectors
are of equal area.

19. If one dart is thrown at the figure above, what is the probability of it hitting the white regions of the inner circle?

    (A) $\frac{1}{9}$

    (B) $\frac{2}{9}$

    (C) $\frac{1}{3}$

    (D) $\frac{4}{9}$

    (E) $\frac{5}{9}$

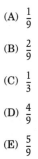

20. The student committee to investigate the missing prom funds is to be made up of four members of the student council. If there are seven members in the student council, then how many different committees are possible?

(A) 840
(B) 210
(C) 120
(D) 35
(E) 24

ANSWERS & EXPLANATIONS

1.   C

The first item is the easiest on a section, and this one is no exception. The only trick is that you have to look at the year *before* the year in the answer choice to tell whether there was a decrease. Consider choice **A**, 1980. You would have to know how many cars were sold in 1979 to say whether 1980 was a better or worse year. For that reason, choice **A** is incorrect. The only two years that see decreases are 1982 and 1985, but since 1985 isn't an answer choice, the answer must be choice **C**, 1982.

2.   D

Here's another straight "Can you use your eyes?" kind of item. There are two ways to approach this item:

1. You can start with the answer choices and check them all out, making notes about how close you think the car sales were in two years.
2. You can start with the graph, come up with an answer, then scan the answer choices to see if it's there.

Option 2 is good because it gives you an aggressive, take-charge attitude that is beneficial when taking a test. The only drawback is that it doesn't always work, because the answer you find might not be one of the choices listed. (Think about the previous item and imagine what it would have been like to decide 1985 was the answer and then hit the answer choices. You would have been disappointed.)

Still, if Option 2 fails, you can always rely on dependable Option 1, so let's try it first. Gazing at the vertical bars and slicing your eye across horizontally, it appears that 1983 and 1985 are very close. 1980 and 1982 are also pretty similar. Looking down at the choices, choice **D** is '83 and '85, and '80 and '82 are not listed. **D**'s your answer.

3. **B**

So long as you keep the Three Ms—mean, median, and mode—straight in your head, you won't stumble on this easy item. To find median, you need to rearrange set A in order from least to greatest.

Current set A: Set A: {6, 8, 3, 2, 3, 5, 9, 5, 12, 3, 9, 1, 1, 6, 7}

Set A after housecleaning: {1, 1, 2, 3, 3, 3, 5, 5, 6, 6, 7, 8, 9, 9, 12}

When writing out the numbers from least to greatest, you might want to cross them out in the original Set A. This lets you keep track of what numbers you've rearranged and which ones you haven't.

There is an odd number (15) of numbers in set A, so the median, or middle, value will be the eighth number. This turns out to be 5, choice **B**.

4. **E**

Because pie charts often show percentages—like this one—they are often accompanied by a real number, such as "Monthly Household Income = $2,400." This allows the test-makers to fashion items like this one, where you have to find the right percentage, then convert this to an actual dollar amount.

The conversion is fairly straightforward. If the mortgage is 33% of the total monthly income and this income is $2,400, then:

$$(33\%)(\$2,400) = (0.33)(\$2,400) = \$792.$$

That's choice **E**.

5. **A**

Here you get your first taste of fiddling with a chart. *Auto Payment* and *Fun* are right next to each other—imagine erasing the line between the two. You would now have a new pie piece. To paraphrase the stem, your goal is to find an old pie piece that is the same size as this new "Auto Payments plus Fun" piece. The answer is literally right next to the new piece, because *Food*, choice **A**, is roughly the same size as the new piece. This shouldn't be surprising because food consists of 26% of the budget and the new piece combines auto (19%) and fun (9%). Together they combine to make 19% + 9% = 28%.

6. **B**

There are two ways to crack this item. You can set up the equation for averages or you can go into the answer choices and start trying out different numbers to see which one satisfies the stem. Because this is only item 6, setting up the equation won't be too hard, but keep in mind that as the items get harder, you're better off solving them using unexpected methods. In other words, this stem is designed to trip up people who set up an equation. Avoiding this route will help you avoid potential distractors.

Let's take choice **C**, 8, and see what average we get:

$$\text{Average} = \frac{\text{sum of elements}}{\text{number of elements}}$$

$$\text{Average} = \frac{9 + 11 + 6 + x + x}{5}$$

$$\text{Average} = \frac{9 + 11 + 6 + 8 + 8}{5}$$

$$\text{Average} = \frac{42}{5}$$

$$\text{Average} = 8.4$$

If $x = 8$ (choice **C**), then we get an average of 8.4. This is not correct, though, because the stem asks for an average of 8. If choice **C** is too large, you can eliminate choices **D** and **E** as well, because they are also going to be too large. This leaves only **A** and **B** as the possible answer.

8.4 is only slightly more than 8, so we need an answer choice that is slightly less than choice **C**. Choice **B**, 7, fits the bill perfectly, whereas choice **A** is much smaller. **B** is your answer. You can double-check this answer if you want, but once you gain enough experience in the way the SAT works, you'll know that this step isn't necessary.

7.   E

Just knowing the definition of *mode* will help you cross out some answer choices. The mode of the set is the number that appears the most. The actual numbers are 5, 8, and 13, with *x* and *y* as two distinct unknowns. The term *distinct* means that *x* and *y* are not the same number. The mode, then, of this set would be any of the real numbers that appears twice as either *x* or *y*. You can cross out choices **B** and **C** because they are not numbers of the set.

You now have a one-in-three shot. The answer has to be 5, 8, or 13. You could set up an equation at this point, but again, don't glibly do things that the item wants you to do.

Look at the numbers 5, 8, and 13. The stem states that the average of set *G* is 6.8. Two of the known numbers (8 and 13) are larger than 6.8. It makes sense that the unknown number would have to be smaller than 6.8 in order to balance out the 8 and 13. That's what averages are all about, isn't it?

You have only one answer choice, 5, that's smaller than 6.8. Pick it.

Yes, you could go through all the math exactly the way the items wants you to, but you'll just end up at choice **E**. It's better to get in the habit of approaching items from an unexpected flank.

8.   E

A probability item rears its ugly head, a clear sign that we have left the Land of the Easy Items and entered the Realm of Medium Difficulty. The deck of cards is divided up evenly between *four* kinds of cards: 10s, Jacks, Queens, and Kings. There's your UNDER number right there: it's 4, the total number of kinds of cards. The stem asks for the probability of NOT drawing a Jack. Only one kind of card is a Jack. The other three are not. Three is your OVER number, then. The probability is 3/4, choice **E**. On this item, the total number of cards didn't come into play, but it was not the toughest probability you'll ever see.

9.   D

Eye and Brain time! This item is very similar to item 1, only this time you have a line graph instead of a bar graph. Using your eyes, you can see that there are two big upward spikes in the graph. March–April is a big one, and so is November–December. But writing the spikes as "March–April" and "November–December" is not exactly accurate, and it confuses things by mentioning two months. The more accurate description is that the two big spikes occur during "March 1st–March 31st and "November 1st–November 30th." This is what the line graph is really describing. Put in this light, March is answer choice **D**, but there is no November answer choice, so **D** must be the correct answer.

10.   **D**

Finding the starting stock price is simple, because the line starts at 50 immediately above January 1st. The endpoint of the line is farther away from the vertical axis denoting dollars, but you can eyeball it and tell that the ending price is above 50 but below 75.

Your eye has done its part. Now it's your brain's turn. Because there was a stock increase, choice **E** is incorrect, so you can cross it out. If the stock had increased by $75, the increase would have been $75 – $50 = $25. Twenty-five dollars is half of $50, so that increase would have been 50%, choice **C**. But you know that the line *doesn't* reach 75, so 50% (choice **C**) is too big. If **C** is too big and **E** is not enough, there's only one answer it can be: choice **D**, 20%.

11.   **A**

This scatterplot graph doesn't feature an overwhelming number of points, which is nice. Primarily, this item hopes to blow your mind with its strangeness. Remember that with a scatterplot, the whole point—get it, *point*—is to find the average trend. The line through all the different points shows this average trend.

For this scatterplot graph, the line would go through that dense mass of points in the middle and should look something like this:

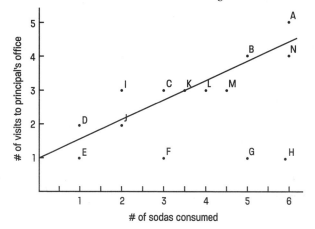

Three of your answer choices—points *F*, *G*, and *H*—are way too low, while point *I* is a little high. Point *K* is right in the thick of things, and that's a good place to be when dealing with scatterplots. Choice **A** is the answer.

12. **A**

As always, you can do the math, or you can try the unconventional road. Taking the unconventional method will get you there safer, but we'll show you how to do the math this time to illustrate all the different ways to get the correct answer.

With the addition of the six new families, there are 14 families total (the new six plus the old eight). The average for this group is $32,000. If the old group of eight averaged $24,000, then the total amount of money they make could be found by multiplying 24,000 by 8. If you make the new average income n, you can say:

$$\text{Average} = \frac{\text{sum of elements}}{\text{number of elements}}$$

$$32,000 = \frac{8(24,000) + 6n}{14}$$

$$448,000 = 8(24,000) + 6n$$

$$448,000 = 192,000 + 6n$$

$$256,000 = 6n$$

$$42,666.67 \approx n$$

That's choice **A**. The unconventional way would have you look over the answer choices and understand how averages work. If six families come in and raise the average income by 1/3 ($24,000 to $32,000), then the new income has to be a bit higher than the current number but not a huge amount. Scanning the answer choices, **C**, **D**, and **E** are all very big. This makes them highly unlikely to be correct. **A** or **B** are the only real possibilities, and **B** is a long shot. **A**'s the answer.

Why is **E** even there? Well, you can see it in the equation line $256,000 = 6n$. If you do the math and forget to divide by 6, you end up with this ridiculous answer choice. Doing the math often leads to distractors, which is why it should be avoided whenever possible. On the grid-in items, sometimes the only way to answer an item is do the math. On multiple-choice items, you often have other methods at your disposal.

13.   **C**

To find the UNDER value, total up the number of candies.

$$\text{Yellow} = 7$$

$$\text{Red} = 3$$

$$\text{Blue} = 5$$

$$\text{Brown} = 5$$

$$\text{Green} = 8$$

$$\text{Total at the start} = 7 + 3 + 5 + 5 + 8 = 28$$

There are 8 green candies, so the OVER on the first grab out of the bag is 8. This gives the first probability of $\frac{8}{28}$. For the second grab out of the bag, you need to remember that one candy has been pulled out, so the UNDER number changes from 28 to 27. There are still 3 reds, so the OVER value is 3. The second probability is $\frac{3}{27}$. Multiplying the two probabilities together will give you:

$$\frac{8}{28} \times \frac{3}{27} = \frac{2}{7} \times \frac{1}{9} = \frac{2}{63}$$

That's choice **C**.

14. **D**

The whole point of most graph items is to freak you out visually. Once you get over the freakiness, the answer is often not too hard to find. On this item, those two cute 16% values hiding in the lower parts of the bell curve are the key to this item. The first 16% shows the percentage of students who scored lower than 61. The second 16% at the far end shows the number of students who scored better than 89. Everyone else scored between a 61 and 89, and you can find this percentage by starting with a 100% and subtracting the two 16% values.

$$100\% - 16\% - 16\% = 68\%$$

There's choice **D**.

15. **B**

You need to use the multiple-choice format to your benefit on this item. Use your eyes and look at the line that shows the hill at its highest. The score there is 75. This means 75 is the mode, because more students scored a 75 than anything else.

Now look at your answer choices. Only choices **A** and **B** have 75 as the mode. You can cross out **C**, **D**, and **E**, leaving you with a 50/50 shot. Speaking of 50/50, you can also see that the line up from 75 evenly divides the curve into two equal parts. This makes 75 the median of the set of scores. This gets rid of choice **A** as an answer, so the correct answer must be **B**.

Mean doesn't even matter. You found the right answer, so move on.

16. C

The last five items are hard for a reason. They have strangely worded stems with multiple steps needed to unlock them. That's just the way it is. Working the last five items is not where you should spend most of your time. Instead, make sure you have the easy and medium items solved correctly, then hope you get a couple of these last Bad Boys.

Once you wade through the stem, you should find that it's a basic factorial item. You start out with six possible first courses, followed by five possible second courses (one less because you have a first course), followed by four possible third courses, and so on. Mathematically, this looks like:

$$6 \times 5 \times 4 \times 3 \times 2 \times 1$$

Now use your trusty calculator and multiply everything together. The product should be 720. This means there are 720 possible combinations, which is choice **C**.

17. C

The answer is not 7.5%. Anyone who approaches an item 17 and thinks the answer can be found by subtracting the 2000 employee benefits percentage (2.5%) from the 1970 employee benefits percentage of 10% needs to go over the Order of Difficulty thing. Hard items are hard for a reason. If they seem very easy, it's because you're falling for a trap. That's how it works, pure and simple.

To tackle this item correctly, you need to find actual cash values for employee benefits in 1970 and 2000. You can't just add or subtract percentages because the amount of money made by the company changed from $12 million to $36 million.

1970 Employee Benefits:

$(10\%)(\$12,000,000) = (0.10)(12,000,000) = \$1,200,000.$

2000 Employee Benefits:

$(2.5\%)(\$36,000,000) = (0.025)(36,000,000) = \$900,000.$

Those are the actual amounts. The decrease is employee benefits, in dollars, was: $1,200,000 – $900,000 = $300,000. This is a percentage decrease of 25%, because $300,000 is 1/4 of $1,200,000. The answer is **C**.

18.   B

Again, you have to find actual number values. You can't go adding and subtracting percentages willy-nilly. First, you have to find out how much each board member made in 1970.

Amount made in 1970:

$$(\text{percentage made by Board})(\text{total profits}) =$$

$$(15\%)(12 \text{ million}) = (0.15)(\$12,000,000) = \$1,800,000.$$

This is the amount made by all eight board members. Each member made about 1/8 of this, or $225,000.

Amount made in 2000:

$$(\text{percentage made by Board})(\text{total profits}) =$$

$$(20\%)(36 \text{ million}) = (0.20)(\$36,000,000) = \$7,200,000.$$

Again, this is the amount made by all of the Board of Directors. Dividing by 8 gives us the average earnings of one board member equals $900,000.

One more computation to go. To find the increase in pay, we must subtract the 1970 value from the 2000 value:

$$\$900,000 - \$225,000 = \$675,000.$$

This is answer choice **B**.

Whew! On hard items, you've got to earn it.

19.   A

If you clutch to the OVER/UNDER method for probability, you have a chance on this one. The goal is to think in terms of area. The UNDER portion is the area of the whole circular dartboard with a radius of 4.

$$\text{Area of circle} = \pi r^2 = \pi 4^2 = 16\pi$$

Doesn't look too promising, does it? Before you abandon all hope, let's look at the inner circle. The odds of hitting the inner circle alone would be computed the same way—by finding the area of the inner circle. But only 4 out of 9 inner circle pie sectors are white, so this number for inner circle area would then have to be multiplied by $\frac{4}{9}$. As ugly as it seems, this is the way to find the OVER value.

$$(\text{area of inner circle})\left(\frac{4}{9}\right) = \text{OVER value}$$
$$(\pi r^2)\left(\frac{4}{9}\right) = (\pi 2^2)\left(\frac{4}{9}\right) = \frac{16\pi}{9}$$

Never let it be said that the SAT doesn't award hard work. When we place the OVER value on top of the UNDER value, we get:

$$\frac{\text{OVER}}{\text{UNDER}} = \frac{\frac{16\pi}{9}}{16\pi} = \left(\frac{16\pi}{9}\right)\left(\frac{1}{16\pi}\right) = \frac{1}{9}$$

When you're dividing with fractions, you have to flip the value in the denominator over and then multiply. This makes 16π become $\frac{1}{16\pi}$, and then the 16πs cancel each other out. The answer is choice **A**.

20.   **A**

If this item is harder than the last one, you know it's going to be a doozy. This is actually a permutation of a factorial, and if you're one of the few people walking around with the formula $_nP_r = \frac{n!}{(n-r)!}$ in your head, then you're in luck. It's what you need to solve this item.

The number n is the total members of the student council, and r is the number of members in the smaller investigation committee. The stem gives us values of $n = 7$ and $r = 4$. Put those into the formula, and you get:

$$_nP_r = \frac{n!}{(n-r)!}$$

$$_nP_r = \frac{7!}{(7-4)!}$$

$$_nP_r = \frac{7!}{3!}$$

$$_nP_r = \frac{7 \times 6 \times 5 \times 4 \times 3 \times 2 \times 1}{3 \times 2 \times 1}$$

$$_nP_r = 7 \times 6 \times 5 \times 4$$

$$_nP_r = 840$$

That's choice **A**. This last item is indicative of how the new SAT will pull out an obscure idea (permutations) in order to make an item very hard to solve.

PRACTICE SET 2: GRID-INS

Questions 1–4 refer to the following set.

Set Q {x, 6, 8, 12, –4, x, 8, 3, x}

1. In set Q, if $x = 7$, what is the average of set Q?

2. What is one possible integer value for x so that the median of set Q is 3?

3. In set Q, if the value of x is 2 greater than the largest numerical value present, what is the range of the set?

4. If the average of set Q is 5, what is the mode of set Q?

Questions 5 and 6 refer to the following graph.

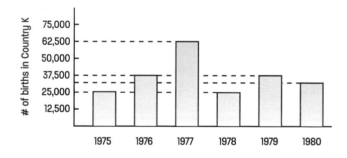

The graph above illustrates the number of births in Country K over a six-year period.

5. In Country K, the greatest percent change—either increase or decrease—for any two consecutive years is equal to what?

6. What is the LEAST percentage change for any two years?

7. Two six-sided dice, numbered 1–6 on each, are thrown simultaneously. What is the probability that the sum of the two sides is greater than 9?

Questions 8 and 9 refer to the following graph.

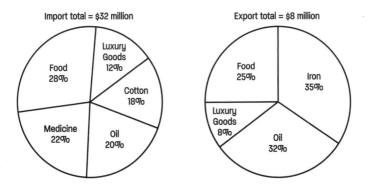

Import total = $32 million

Export total = $8 million

8. The amount imported in food is how much greater, in millions of dollars, than the entire amount of goods exported?

9. What is the change in dollars between the amount of medicine imported and the amount of iron exported? Grid your answer in millions of dollars.

10. The average of five positive integers is 6. No more than two numbers are the same. All numbers are greater than 3 and less than 10. What is one possible value of the mode?

Questions 11, 12, and 13 refer to the following graph.

Wildlife in the African Savanna

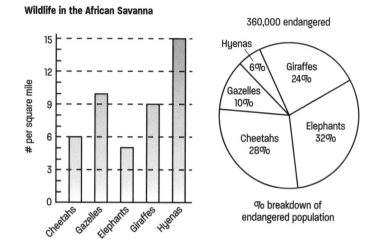

360,000 endangered

% breakdown of
endangered population

11. According to the graph, what fraction of the entire population for one square mile is composed of giraffes?

12. If there is a total of 180,000 gazelles in the savanna, then how many per square mile are endangered?

13. If 6 hyenas per square mile are endangered, then how many hyenas, in thousands, are there in the savanna?

14. Fonzy is sitting down to a meal of macaroni and cheese. He has four different condiments to choose from: ketchup, picante sauce, Tabasco sauce, and ranch dressing. If he is going to use at least one and no more than four, then how many different combinations of condiments does he have to choose from?

15. Ben decides to get an ice cream cone. He is going to choose two toppings out of an available six. Ben also has a choice between a plain cone and a waffle cone. If Ben chooses vanilla ice cream, how many different combinations of toppings and cones does Ben have to choose from?

ANSWERS & EXPLANATIONS

1.   6

There would be many different ways to attack this item if it were in the multiple-choice section. With grid-ins, you're forced to approach the item using the Math Path. Sigh. Grid-ins are no fun.

After you place everything into the equation for mean average, all you have to do is solve the item by manipulating the equation correctly. The missing piece is the average:

$$\text{Average} = \frac{x + 6 + 8 + 12 + (-4) + x + 8 + 3 + x}{9}$$

$$\text{Average} = \frac{7 + 6 + 8 + 12 + (-4) + 7 + 8 + 3 + 7}{9}$$

$$\text{Average} = \frac{54}{9} = 6$$

2.   3

When dealing with median, it always helps to line things up. Here's set Q without the three xs:

$$-4, 3, 6, 8, 8, 12$$

As you can see, the 3 is way to the left of the list, and for it to be the median, it needs to be in the middle. To get 3 into the middle, you would need a value for x less than 3. Any integer less than 3 would work, but on grid-in items, there's no way to grid in negative numbers, so this constrains things a bit. Your best answers are 0, 1, and 2. If you picked $x = 1$, for instance, your set would look like:

$$-4, 1, 1, 1, 3, 6, 8, 8, 12$$

That puts 3 in the middle. You can even have $x = 3$, which would make 3 not only the median but the mode as well.

3.   18

The range of a set is the difference between the largest numerical value and the smallest. In set Q, 12 is the largest number visible, but the stem states that x is 2 greater than this value, so $x = 14$. The smallest value is -4, so the range would be:

$$14 - (-4) = 18$$

Grid that in.

4. **4**

This item will look a lot like the first item, only here the missing piece is not the average but the value of x.

$$\text{Average} = \frac{x + 6 + 8 + 12 + (-4) + x + 8 + 3 + x}{9}$$

$$5 = \frac{33 + 3x}{9}$$

$$(9)5 = \frac{33 + 3x}{9}(9)$$

$$45 = 33 + 3x$$

$$12 = 3x$$

$$\frac{12}{3} = 4$$

Because there are three xs in the equation, this value of x is the mode for the set—no other number appears as often.

5. **66.67**

The drop from 1977 to 1978 sure looks the steepest, but it might not be the steepest in terms of percentage. The difference in numbers between the two years is $62,500 - 25,000 = 37,500$. What percent of 62,500 is 37,500? The answer is:

$$\frac{n}{100}(62,500) = (37,500)$$

$$625n = 37,500$$

$$n = 60$$

Sixty percent is a steep drop. However, we should check the percentage increase from 1976 to 1977 before moving on. Even though the actual number of births is less, the percentage change may be greater.

To understand why this is, consider a room with only one person in it. If another person enters, the occupancy of the room increases by 100%. Now imagine a room with 100 people in it. If 10 people enter, the occupancy increases by 10%. Even though more actual people entered, the percentage change was less since there were more people to begin with.

The difference in births between 1976 and 1977 is: 62,500 – 37,500 = 25,000. What percent of 37,500 is 25,000? The answer is:

$$\frac{n}{100}(37,500) = 25,000$$

$$375n = 25,000$$

$$n \approx 66.67$$

There's the real answer. The big drop-off between 1977 and 1978 is like a cliff. If you weren't looking for a percentage change, you would have fallen right over it.

6.   0

Here's an item meant to trick your eye again. Between 1979 and 1980, there's an ever-so-slight drop of 2,500 births. Your eye would see this slight drop and say, "That's the smallest drop." This is true, but it is only true for consecutive years. The stem says "any two years." The nonconsecutive years 1976 and 1979 had the same amount of births. The percentage between these two years is, therefore, zero. This is the smallest change, smaller even than whatever slight decrease occurred between 1979 and 1980. The grid-in answer for this item is 0.

7.   1/6

Determining the UNDER portion of the probability is easier, so let's start there. If there are two dice with six sides, then the total number of probabilities is (6)(6) = 36. That's the bottom part; now on to the top. Throwing a number that will be greater than 9 isn't easy. In fact, here are the only ways that could happen:

Ways to Throw Higher Than a 9

First Throw	Second Throw
4	6
5	5
5	6
6	4

Ways to Throw Higher Than a 9	
6	5
6	6

Count up the number of different ways. There are six different ways, so that's your OVER number. The probability is $\frac{6}{36}$, which simplifies to $\frac{1}{6}$.

8. **0.96**

The entire amount exported appears above the second pie chart as $8 million. To figure out the amount of food imported, multiply the percent spent on food by the total of $32 million:

$$(28\% \text{ imported food})(\$32 \text{ million import total}) =$$

$$(0.28)(\$32,000,000) = \$8,960,000$$

The amount imported in food is greater than total exports by:

$$\$8,960,000 - \$8,000,000 = \$960,000$$

Don't try to grid this huge number in, however. Recall that the stem asks for the answer in millions of dollars. In millions of dollars, $960,000 = 0.96.

Kind of tricky, eh? Welcome to the grid-in section.

9. **4.24**

We hope you are getting the hang of these percent items and would never, ever consider simply adding or subtracting percentages. You need to find the real numbers:

Amount of medicine imported:

$$(22\% \text{ of total})(\text{import total}) =$$

$$(0.22)(\$32 \text{ million}) = \$7.04 \text{ million}$$

Amount of iron exported:

$$(35\% \text{ of total})(\text{export total}) =$$

$$(0.35)(\$8 \text{ million}) = \$2.8 \text{ million}$$

Now you need to subtract the two real values. Because the answer is in millions of dollars, there's no need to write out 7.04 million as 7,040,000. In fact, that would only cause trouble.

$$\$7.04 - \$2.8 = \$4.24 \text{ million.}$$

Grid in the number 4.24.

10. **5**

This item seems tough, but the word *possible* makes things a bit easier. You don't have to figure out a single solution. If you try something and it works, then that's a possible answer.

Why not try a number next to 6, such as 5? If 5 were the mode, it would appear twice, and no other number could appear more than once. This will help once we look at the formula for averages and determine what our missing piece is for this item:

$$\text{Average} = \frac{\text{sum of elements}}{\text{total number of elements}}$$
$$6 = \frac{\text{sum of elements}}{5}$$
$$30 = \text{sum of the elements}$$

If two of the elements are 5, then the other three elements have to equal 20 because $30 - 2(5) = 30 - 10 = 20$. The question now becomes, Can you think of three distinct integers greater than 3 but less than 10 that sum to 20? If you can, you've found a possible answer.

This will take some scratch work. You might get frustrated. If so, try a different number as the mode that appears twice. If you stick with it, though, you should come up with:

$$7 + 9 + 4 = 20$$

If the set of numbers was 4, 5, 5, 7, and 9, the mode would be 5 and the average would be 6. So 5 is one possible answer.

11. **1/5**

The danger on this item is using the wrong graph. You might have a great urge to look at the pie chart and pluck that 24% giraffe number out. Don't. The stem talks about the population per square mile, so the bar graph must be used. To find out what fraction of the population per square mile is giraffes, you need to determine the total number of animals per square mile. From the bar graph, this would be:

Cheetahs = 6

Gazelles = 10

Elephants = 5

Giraffes = 9

Hyenas = 15

Total number of animals = 45

Man, that place is crawling with hyenas. But don't worry about that for now. Take the total number of animals and place the number of giraffes per square miles on top of it. This will give you the fraction the item asks for:

$$\frac{9 \text{ giraffes per square mile}}{45 \text{ total animals per square mile}} = \frac{9}{45} = \frac{1}{5}$$

12. **2**

Both graphs come into play on this one, signaling that we're in Hard Grid-In Territory. First, use the pie chart to determine the number of endangered gazelles. If there are 360,000 total endangered animals and 10% of these are gazelles, then the actual number of endangered gazelles is:

$$(10\%)(360{,}000) = (0.10)(360{,}000) = 36{,}000.$$

The stem states that the total population of gazelles is 180,000, so obviously not all gazelles are in trouble. In fact, only $\frac{36,000}{180,000} = 0.2 = 20\%$ of them are in trouble. If 20% of all gazelles are endangered and there are 10 gazelles per square mile (from the bar chart), then 20% of these 10 gazelles are endangered. 20% of 10 is 2, your grid-in answer.

13. **54**

This item is like the last one in reverse. There are 15 hyenas per square mile, and 6 of them are endangered. That means $\frac{6}{15} = 0.4 = 40\%$ of all hyenas are in trouble. Going over to the pie chart, you find the actual number of endangered hyenas is:

(6%)(360,000 endangered animals) = (0.06)(360,000) = 21,600.

Now you have the number and percentage of endangered hyenas. You must now ask yourself, "21,600 is 40% of what number?" In Mathspeak, this is:

$$21,600 = (40\%)(n)$$

$$21,600 = 0.4n$$

$$54,000 = n$$

There are 54,000 hyenas on the savanna. In thousands, you would grid in 54.

14. **15**

You can whip out that freaky-deaky permutation of a factorial formula, but even that won't cleanly get you through this item. The best way might be to go low-tech: list out the different combinations. There aren't as many as you might think:

Using all four condiments: 1 possibility

Using only one condiment: 4 possibilities,
because there are four condiments

Using three condiments: 4 possibilities (all three minus one of them)

Using two condiments: 6 possibilities (K-P, K-T, K-R, P-T, P-R, R-T)

Adding up all the possibilities gives you 15 possible combinations. There's your answer.

15. **60**

Here's where that funky permutation formula comes in. Because Ben is going to choose two toppings out of six, you have:

$$_nP_r = \frac{n!}{(n-r)!}$$

$$_nP_r = \frac{6!}{(6-2)!}$$

$$_nP_r = \frac{6!}{4!}$$

$$_nP_r = \frac{6 \times 5 \times 4 \times 3 \times 2 \times 1}{4 \times 3 \times 2 \times 1}$$

$$_nP_r = 6 \times 5$$

$$_nP_r = 30$$

But that covers only the toppings. There are two kinds of cones, so you must multiply 30 by 2 to show that all those different combinations could be placed on either a plain cone or a waffle cone. The correct answer is 60.

SPARKNOTES
Power Tactics for the New SAT

The Critical Reading Section

Reading Passages

Sentence Completions

The Math Section

Algebra

Data Analysis, Statistics & Probability

Geometry

Numbers & Operations

The Writing Section

The Essay

*Multiple-Choice Questions: Identifying Sentence Errors,
Improving Sentences, Improving Paragraphs*

The New SAT

Test-Taking Strategies

Vocabulary Builder